Cleaning Business

TABLE OF CONTENTS

WHO SHOULD BUY THIS BOOK --- 6

INTRODUCTION --- 7

CHAPTER 1: THE IMPORTANCE OF CLEANING AND HYGIENE --------- 10

CHAPTER 2: WHAT IS TARGETED HYGIENE AND WHY DO WE NEED IT? -- 13

CHAPTER 3: HOW TO DEAL WITH THE DIRTIEST SPOTS AROUND THE HOUSE AND WORKPLACE --- 17
- The 10 dirtiest places in your home - which deserve special attention ------ 17
- The dirtiest places at work -- 19
- The 5 dirtiest places at work are listed below: ---------------------------- 21

CHAPTER 4: ROOM BY ROOM CLEANING ----------------------------- 23
- How to clean your bathroom --- 23
- How To Clean The Kitchen Thoroughly ------------------------------- 25
- How to clean the bedroom: practical tips -------------------------------- 29
- Cleaning the Living Room -- 33

CHAPTER 5: PEOPLE MOST EFFECTED BY THE LACK OF CLEANLINESS? -- 37
- PREGNANT WOMEN -- 37
- ELDERLY AND / OR SICK PEOPLE -- 40
- BABIES AND YOUNG CHILDREN -- 43
- PETS AND HYGIENE -- 47

CHAPTER 6: WHY USE A "CLEANING COMPANY"? ----------------------- 49
- What are the services offered by a cleaning company -------------------- 49

The cleaning of the condominiums --- 50
Industrial cleaning --- 50
Cleaning and maintenance of green areas --- 51
10 good reasons to contact a cleaning company ---------------------------------- 51

CHAPTER 7: BUSINESS PLAN --- 57
Why is the business plan so important? -- 58
2. Canvas and pitch deck as alternatives to the business plan ------------------ 64
3. Content and structure of the business plan -------------------------------------- 65

CHAPTER 8: THE BUSINESS MODEL CANVAS ------------------------------ 82
The 10 most important questions about the business model canvas --------- 83
Advantages and disadvantages of a business model canvas -------------------- 85

CHAPTER 9: THE PERFECT PITCH DECK --------------------------------------- 87
1. Frequently asked questions about the pitch deck ------------------------------- 87
2. Content and structure -- 89
3. Avoid mistakes in the pitch deck -- 92
4. Pitch deck templates, patterns, and tools --- 94
6. Pitch deck ready - what now? --- 96
7. Conclusion: present correctly -- 96

CHAPTER 10: BUSINESS IDEA, OFFER AND TARGET GROUP ----------- 97

CHAPTER 11: MARKET ANALYSIS AND COMPETITION ANALYSIS ---- 105

CHAPTER 12: MARKET SIZE AND VOLUME ------------------------------- 110
Determine market size and volume -- 110

CHAPTER 13: MARKET DYNAMICS --- 113

CHAPTER 14: MARKET POTENTIAL --- 116
3 steps: How to determine the market potential ------------------------------------ 117
Market Potential: A Simple Calculation -- 117
1. Trends influence the market potential --- 118

2. Dependence on the services life cycle and market potential --------------- 118
3. Theoretically possible market size, the market potential ------------------- 119

CHAPTER 15: COMPETITIVE ANALYSIS AND COMPETITION ANALYSIS -- 121
2 steps to the competition and competition analysis ---------------------------- 121
1. Analyze the competition -- 122
2. Competitor analysis: who are your competitors? ---------------------------- 123
Market research: Basis for the competition analysis ----------------------------- 125

CHAPTER 16: MARKET SHARE: METHODS AND FORMULAS ---------- 127
1. What does market share mean? --- 127
Absolute and relative market share: what is the difference? ----------------- 128
2. Calculate market share: method, and formula -------------------------------- 129
3. Common questions about market share ------------------------------------- 131
4. Conclusion --- 133

CHAPTER 17: COMPANY GOALS AND OBJECTIVES---------------------- 135
Corporate goals --- 136

CHAPTER 18: CORPORATE STRATEGY: HOW TO ACHIEVE YOUR GOALS --- 138

CHAPTER 19: LAW AND TAXATION--- 141
What permits do you need for your job? -- 141

CHAPTER 20: OPERATIONAL ORGANIZATION ----------------------- 144
Business organization as a success factor for companies ---------------------- 144
Mandatory components in the operational organization --------------------- 145

CHAPTER 21: FINANCIAL PLANNING FOR THE BUSINESS-------------- 148

CHAPTER 22: SWOT ANALYSIS -- 156
What is the SWOT analysis? -- 156

4

1. The components of the SWOT analysis --- 157
2. How to easily create your SWOT analysis --- 158

CHAPTER 23: THE EXECUTIVE SUMMARY --- 166

CHAPTER 24: SUM UP ALL TOGETHER.......SET UP YOUR CLEANING COMPANY --- 170

CHAPTER 25: BECOME A SELF-EMPLOYED CLEANING CONTRACTOR --- 184

Pros and cons of starting a cleaning business as a self-employed person - 186

CHAPTER 26: SELF-EMPLOYED AS A GENERAL CLEANER --- 189

CHAPTER 27: BECOMING SELF-EMPLOYED AS A BUILDING CLEANER --- 194

Becoming self-employed as a building cleaner: an overview of key success factors --- 198

CHAPTER 28: SELF-EMPLOYED AS A WINDOW CLEANER --- 200

CHAPTER 29: BECOME SELF-EMPLOYED AS A GRAFFITI CLEANER --- 206

Summary & FAQ on the business idea 'become self-employed as a graffiti cleaner' --- 213

CONCLUSION --- 215

WHO SHOULD BUY THIS BOOK

Cleaning our surroundings has always been a sacred ritual in almost all religions. It has taken different forms according to traditions. With the commercialization of various activities, cleaning is no exception. Our busy and hectic schedules have forced many of us to contract the services of professional cleaning services.

This book is aimed at both classes, people who want to take up the traditional cleaning services themselves, and those who want to hire professional cleaning services.

Above all, it is for those, who want to start a cleaning business themselves. We have detailed the whole process in the form of a business plan, to take you step by step through the whole process, from inception of idea, gathering finances, forming business strategies to final creation of the company.

Although, we have referred all our business plan steps to the creation of a cleaning company, but they can be adapted to any other business as well.

For our readers who prefer a simpler method than the creation of business plan, we have added two additional chapters, of Business Model Canvas and Pitch Deck.

In the end, we have added different models of setting up cleaning business, from general contractor to building cleaner, window cleaner, and graffiti cleaner.

Hence, this book acts as a complete reference on the subject of cleaning and cleaning business.

INTRODUCTION

Cleaning and hygiene are physiological practices that by their nature cannot be separated from ecological ones. They have the same purposes: harmony, beauty, health.

If there was a lack (among the various shortcomings that emerged) the attention and, consequently, the habit towards hygiene (handwashing is a symbol of this lacuna) probably lacked the motivation, the stimulus to carry out a practice considered not too important, not vital and natural. From the anthropological point of view, cleanliness with its opposite, dirt, are considered completely cultural aspects, therefore relating to historical periods, traditions, rites, and the fear of contamination.

Cleaning calls for care, protection, attention, dedication, relationship. Cleaning also calls for order, organization, planning, in everyday life.

If from this time of great trial we come out with a new culture of cleaning that allows us to implement healthy habits for ourselves, for the home, and for the environment (creating a healthy daily routine) we can all start the change of course together, that depends mainly on us, on our choices, on our behavior.

Clean, sanitize, disinfect, sanitize. Verbs that have invaded the daily news of recent months and that have brought back the practice of cleaning.

The epidemic that has blocked millions of people at home, in some way, has given rise to the "rebirth" of this personal and domestic activity which has suddenly been positioned on the podium of our daily life.

Covid-19 has forced us to have greater regard for health and hygiene aspects including those related to the cleaning of our homes, offices, and other places of gathering. Attention to eliminating viruses, bacteria, and other invisible threats has been a priority to try to protect our human health.

What did this sudden and unexpected change in our relationship with cleaning entail?

Excess of hygiene. Using massive and reckless bactericides and disinfectants.

" The abuse of disinfectants has already had a clear impact on our health. Since the beginning of the Covid-19 emergency, counseling for intoxication from the use of disinfectants has increased by 63% for adults and 135% for children under five. The environmental impact is another aspect that should not be underestimated: sodium hypochlorite (bleach) has very negative and persistent effects on aquatic environments, where it damages algae and fish and interferes on the food chain, exerting effects that last over time. Both medical-surgical aids and biocidal substances indistinctly attack all the bacteria they encounter, exerting a bad impact on the environment.

During the quarantine, many thought that it was essential to disinfect domestic environments with extraordinary cleaning compared to that practiced pre-covid-19.

Carefully cleaning each surface properly can be useful, but in the same way, it is essential to understand how to do it with the use of suitable servicess. With the correct precautions and the right precautions, there is no need to disinfect or sanitize the rooms, just perform normal daily cleaning correctly. The requirement is different in the case in which there is an infected person in the house, in that case, it is necessary to follow the guidelines of the National Institute of Health.

We have increased hygiene & cleaning routines because we are motivated and stimulated to protect our health and that of our loved ones, rediscovering that hygiene and preventive medicine (defined as the science and art of preventing disease to promote health and well-being) allow us to extend the life and promote health through organized efforts and informed choices in society. The public health becomes acting all adequately to threats.

What lessons can we inherit so as not to nullify the sacrifices due to the crisis experienced due to Covid-19? What happened in this historical passage has put a strain on us, but it also offers us the opportunity of awareness, of awareness, of resilient transformation. Now is the time to learn and responsibly assume habits and behaviors useful for our health and that of others and the environment.

Rediscovering the culture of cleaning is essential.

CHAPTER 1

THE IMPORTANCE OF CLEANING AND HYGIENE

Did you know that 89% of consumers * in the world, feel safe and reassured when their home is clean? Don't take your health for granted. The cleanliness of our apartments and good hygiene habits are of crucial importance for our health and well-being. A good, safe, and sustainable implementation does not have to be a chore either. Good habits are essential to our health.

First, let us describe what we mean when we talk about cleaning and hygiene.

Cleaning and hygiene - what do these terms mean?

Cleaning is the mechanical or chemical removal of dirt and impurities from an object, a surface, or the human body. Usually, cleaning with soap or detergent and then rinsing with water is sufficient to remove any visible dirt and allergens. Cleaning also reduces the number of microorganisms on hands, surfaces, and tissues.

Disinfection is the targeted use of a disinfectant to prevent the spread of infection in situations where there is a high risk of harmful germs being transmitted (e.g. when someone is infected or susceptible to infection). These servicess prevent the infection from spreading by deactivating or killing pathogens.

Hygiene: describes the activities that maintain or promote human health. The cleaning and - if necessary - disinfection of surfaces, hands, devices, surroundings, and objects of personal use contribute to hygiene to interrupt the chain of infection. Other hygiene measures include maintaining a certain distance from sick people.

Cleaning and hygiene at home - basic principles

We clean our home because we like to live in comfortable surroundings. But when we clean our home, it also helps maintain our health.

Regular cleaning makes our home look clean and smells good. This gives us a sense of well-being that helps maintain good health.

Regular cleaning reduces the amount of "dirt" and vermin, such as dust mites, lice, and the like, that can be detrimental to our health. For example, allergens in dust can trigger allergies such as asthma.

Regular cleaning to remove dust, dirt, and food residues has a preventive effect against mice, cockroaches, etc. in the apartment.

Regularly cleaning bed linen prevents bed bug problems.

Regular cleaning reduces the number of fungi that can grow in damp areas in the kitchen, bathroom, and toilet and cause respiratory problems.

Measures such as cleaning, disinfection, and heat treatment prevent the spread of harmful germs and thus protect against infectious diseases.

For measures 1 to 5 above, cleaning is carried out daily or weekly to bring these potential hazards to the lowest possible level. However, cleaning to prevent infection is different.

Protection against harmful microbes through targeted hygiene

Did you know that a clean home does not mean that it is free of potentially harmful microbes that keep getting into the environment, e.g. B. from the people and animals living there, and the food that is prepared? These microbes are invisible and you cannot clean your home to free them from microbes.

The effective way to protect your home from harmful microbes is to use proper hygiene measures in those situations where they are most likely to spread. We call this "targeted hygiene".

CHAPTER 2

WHAT IS TARGETED HYGIENE AND WHY DO WE NEED IT?

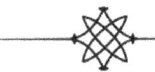

Introducing targeted hygiene measures in your home is the best way to ensure that you are doing your best to protect yourself and your family from infectious diseases.

Targeted hygiene makes it possible to improve protection against harmful microbes while preserving beneficial microbes. We need them to build a healthy microbiome in our intestines, in the airways and the mouth, and on our skin. The risk of developing allergies or other diseases is reduced.

The key to targeted hygiene is to focus on breaking the chain of infection. This is very different from the traditional notion that hygiene means getting rid of the dirt that is mainly home to harmful microbes. The main sources of harmful microbes are other people, contaminated food and water, and pets.

Break the chain of infection to prevent harmful microbes from spreading.

Harmful microbes enter the home mainly through people or pets, contaminated food or water. They are given off constantly and then spread through carriers such as hands, toilets, towels, etc. We can be infected by these microbes by e.g. For example, by touching an infected surface and then touching our mouth, nose, or eyes, or by eating food that has been contaminated by touching it with contaminated hands. This is known as the "chain of infection". For an infection to spread, all links in the "chain of infection" must be present. So if we remove one of the links in the chain, the infection cannot spread.

At home, hygiene measures serve to prevent the further spread of harmful microbes by breaking this chain of infection.

There are some types of microbes that are known to be potentially harmful to health (e.g., some gut bacteria) that can permanently colonize and multiply in areas of stagnant water, such as B. Sink/bath/shower drains, under the flushing rim of the toilet and in wet cleaning rags and sponges. These aren't usually harmful, but they can pose a risk to people with compromised immune systems.

When do you need to use targeted hygiene?

Targeted hygiene means focusing hygiene measures on those times when harmful microbes are most likely to spread from the sources mentioned above. These times include:

- Contact with food
- Eating with your hands
- Using the toilet or changing a baby
- Coughing, sneezing, and blowing your nose
- Touching surfaces that are frequently touched by others
- Dealing with and washing dirty clothes and laundry
- Taking care of pets
- Handling and disposal of garbage
- Taking care of an infected family member.

In these nine situations, you need to apply hygiene measures like hand washing, surface cleaning, etc. to the critical surfaces that are most likely to spread harmful microbes (so-called critical control points). In all nine risk situations, the hands must be hygienically clean, but this also applies to surfaces that come into contact with food and cleaning rags. Harmful microbes can also be transmitted through clothing and bed linen, bathrooms, showers and sinks, and occasionally through floors and furniture.

However, we should be aware that while daily or weekly cleaning of our living spaces can help prevent the spread of infections, this contribution is relatively small compared to the hygiene measures that must be carried out in important critical situations to protect us from contact with harmful microbes.

How can the chain of infection be broken?

The purpose of a hygiene measure is to reduce the number of harmful microbes on hands, surfaces, and fabrics to a level that is harmless to health. This can be achieved by:

Removal of the microbes from the surfaces - with cleaning agents (e.g. cleaning agents or soap) and cleaning utensils with water. Rinsing under running, clean water is an important step in this process.

Killing the microbes on the surfaces in question using servicess/processes such as heating (e.g. by washing at higher temperatures), disinfectants, hand disinfectants.

In many or most situations, cleaning, followed by rinsing and drying, is sufficient to prevent the infection from spreading. However, there are some situations where cleaning followed by disinfection may be required, such as: For example, using hand sanitizer when we don't have access to soap and water or cleaning surfaces that cannot be wiped off thoroughly.

Hand hygiene is the most important hygiene practice and plays a central role in all nine risk situations described above.

To ensure that your hands are hygienically clean, always lather your hands thoroughly, rinse them well under running, clean water, and then dry them thoroughly. Wet hands absorb microbes faster than dry hands. If you have no way of using running water and a towel, use hand sanitizer.

Targeted hygiene is an important part of sustainable hygiene as it avoids the excessive use of cleaning servicess. It also ensures the judicious use of disinfectants, which can help avoid antibiotic resistance.

CHAPTER 3

HOW TO DEAL WITH THE DIRTIEST SPOTS AROUND THE HOUSE AND WORKPLACE

Dirt hides in unexpected places, like the remote. Find out where else it can be and how to clean it. You will be surprised!

Remote controls, faucets, handles, and light switches are places in the house that you never imagined cleaning? Not even a washcloth? It is better to rethink. They are on the list of the dirtiest places in the house. See below the corners of the house where dirt accumulates and you never imagined. And follow the tips on how to clean them.

The 10 dirtiest places in your home - which deserve special attention

1. Faucets

Right where the water comes out. Probably, if you do not clean the area, you will find it with black dirt. And can you imagine brushing your teeth with the water that comes out of there? Then, every two months, remove the mouth from the tap and soak it in vinegar for at least 15 minutes. Brush all parts with a toothbrush to remove any remaining residue and put it back in place.

2. Handles and switches

Imagine the light switches, cabinet handles, and the refrigerator door ... They are usually forgotten when cleaning, but they contain a lot of germs and bacteria because we touch them all the time. Clean them with a microfiber cloth moistened with cleaning servicess and do not forget them in the kitchen cleaning routine.

3. On top of kitchen cabinets

This part of the house is almost no-man's-land, and you can find everything there, among dust and rodent feces. Few people remember to clean this area, but it is necessary, once a month, to climb a ladder and remove all the dirt from there. And it should be the first place to be cleaned, if dust and other things fall from up there, you haven't cleaned the bottom yet.

4. Bathtub

Any water that remains there can generate mold, fungi, and bacteria. The bathtub must be dried after each use and needs to be disinfected regularly.

5. Inside the refrigerator

Leftovers from forgotten meals, rotting fruits, and vegetables, sticky packages, all of this mix in a space accessed by several hands daily. This makes the area one of the dirtiest in the house - the same goes for the microwave. When cleaning, it is best to avoid using chemicals. Remove the shelves and clean with a mixture of hot water and a liquid detergent. Dry them well and return them to the refrigerator.

6. Kitchen sink

Thanks to the mixture of pieces of food and a humid environment, your kitchen sink can be dirtier than the bathroom. Wash it with soap and water daily and disinfect once or twice a week.

7. The walls around the toilet

You think it is bad, but it is worse than you can imagine. The walls must be cleaned with disinfectants. Spray the services and let it sit for a few minutes to eliminate the bacteria. Then wipe with a damp cloth.

8. Remote control

Dirty hands pick up the remote controls many times a day. And it is very rare for anyone to remember to clean them. Use a disinfectant to clean objects frequently. To remove the dirt between the buttons, use a cotton swab dipped in alcohol.

9. Around the stove

It is very common to drop things between the stove and the counter next to it, or the wall behind it. With the heat that is around the place, it creates an environment very favorable to the proliferation of germs and bacteria. Clean the area frequently, removing the stove and spraying disinfectant on the walls, the floor, and the appliance itself.

10. Inside the toothbrush holder

They stay moist and accumulate a lot of dirt. It is important to use accessories that can be cleaned frequently. Dip the glass in a mixture of warm water and bleach for 30 minutes. Then, immerse in clean water for another 30 minutes to remove all residues.

The dirtiest places at work

The place where we work and spend most of our day, if well organized, clean, and tidy, has a positive effect on our efficiency, our performance, and morale.

Countless researches show that having a clean and organized office increases servicesivity for the well-being that comes in the absence of allergies, irritation, or infections, and for the greater concentration that speeds up the completion of an assignment.

Having a clean and sanitized office is also fundamental for an economic factor: employees' sick leave is reduced without compromising company servicesivity.

Furthermore, as a meeting and representation place, a clean office will also be favorably received by customers or other external people who frequent it.

An American company specializing in cleaning and sanitation has analyzed about 5 thousand workstations in call centers, manufacturing companies, offices of various types, with a tool that detects the presence of germs and bacteria and calculates the levels of ATP (adenosine triphosphate), drawing up finally a ranking of the dirtiest places and objects in the office.

Sometimes the dirtiest places at work don't even appear to be. However, the dirt that most concerns us here is not visual, but hygienic. Germs are an important type of dirt to keep in mind, and you should not neglect their cleaning and proper disinfection of parts of your office that are in constant contact with many people.

Contrary to what we might think, the dirtiest place in the offices is not the bathroom but the room used for relaxing breaks: the handle of the door of the kitchens or break areas becomes full of impurities and bacteria of all kinds, the handle of the microwave oven, the handle and the inside of the refrigerator, the buttons to press to buy snacks or coffee have excessive traces of adenosine triphosphate (ATP), at risk of transmitting diseases.

On the desk, however, the dirtiest object is the PC keyboard: research has shown that it can be even dirtier than the toilet seat.

The unsuspected ones are followed by the mouse, the telephone receiver and the smartphones, the photocopier keys, the elevator buttons, but also the air conditioners, the curtains and the chairs of each station are real receptacles of bacteria, to which we never think of and which are not cleaned properly and regularly: it is enough for a single person with the flu to touch one of these objects, says the research coordinator, for the virus to spread very easily.

The 5 dirtiest places at work are listed below:

1. Door handles and appliances

If one of the most effective ways to prevent contamination and infection due to germs is to wash your hands, it is because there is a good reason for that. Doorknobs are one of the dirtiest places at work, especially the interaction areas like the canopy, which are full of germs. Now the question remains: when cleaning is done in your company, are the handles cleaned and disinfected?

2. Elevator buttons and stair railings

Again, the dirtiest places at work are the easiest to forget when cleaning. And again, although they may appear not to be dirty, they need to be cleaned and disinfected frequently.

Elevator and handrail buttons are used every day, by all workers, so when you next office cleaning has this in mind.

3. Keyboards and phones

Let's start with the first. Keyboards end up accumulating dirt over time. Whether it's dirt that we see with the naked eye, like crumbs or dust, or the germs that we inevitably carry in our hands. Once a week, clean your computer keyboard. Use a brush to remove physical dirt and a vacuum cleaner. Then put some disinfectant on a cloth and clean the keyboard.

As for telephones, the problem becomes greater when they are shared. In addition to being more conducive to the accumulation of dust, the germs that are in the hands, or expelled through the mouth when we speak, end up getting stuck. Never forget to clean and disinfect it regularly, also preferably once a week.

4. Coffee machines, water, or the coffee cups and glasses of water themselves

In many companies, the employee brings his cup of coffee and uses the company's machine to drink his espresso. The same with water. This would even be a good step to avoid more dirt and is, above all, a more sustainable action. The problem is that it is very easy to pass the bacteria from the cups to the coffee or water machines. Even if it is the company that supplies the cups, this will not solve the problem.

When cleaning in the office, disinfect all beverage machines and, if applicable, the cups provided to employees.

5. Keys, switches, and handles

When we leave our desk or office, other locations lend themselves to the proliferation of bacteria and germs.

Let's talk, for example, of the common areas where we find coffee machines, vending machines, microwaves, and water dispensers, all strictly equipped with buttons and/or handles and all in common use. Greater use by more people, therefore, implies a higher concentration of germs.

This is why it is important to contact a professional cleaning company, whose staff knows the less " obvious " areas to be cleaned completely and manages to sanitize the environment correctly, with the right servicess and a working method effective.

of and which are not cleaned properly and regularly: it is enough for a single person with the flu to touch one of these objects, says the research coordinator, for the virus to spread very easily.

The 5 dirtiest places at work are listed below:

1. Door handles and appliances

If one of the most effective ways to prevent contamination and infection due to germs is to wash your hands, it is because there is a good reason for that. Doorknobs are one of the dirtiest places at work, especially the interaction areas like the canopy, which are full of germs. Now the question remains: when cleaning is done in your company, are the handles cleaned and disinfected?

2. Elevator buttons and stair railings

Again, the dirtiest places at work are the easiest to forget when cleaning. And again, although they may appear not to be dirty, they need to be cleaned and disinfected frequently.

Elevator and handrail buttons are used every day, by all workers, so when you next office cleaning has this in mind.

3. Keyboards and phones

Let's start with the first. Keyboards end up accumulating dirt over time. Whether it's dirt that we see with the naked eye, like crumbs or dust, or the germs that we inevitably carry in our hands. Once a week, clean your computer keyboard. Use a brush to remove physical dirt and a vacuum cleaner. Then put some disinfectant on a cloth and clean the keyboard.

As for telephones, the problem becomes greater when they are shared. In addition to being more conducive to the accumulation of dust, the germs that are in the hands, or expelled through the mouth when we speak, end up getting stuck. Never forget to clean and disinfect it regularly, also preferably once a week.

4. Coffee machines, water, or the coffee cups and glasses of water themselves

In many companies, the employee brings his cup of coffee and uses the company's machine to drink his espresso. The same with water. This would even be a good step to avoid more dirt and is, above all, a more sustainable action. The problem is that it is very easy to pass the bacteria from the cups to the coffee or water machines. Even if it is the company that supplies the cups, this will not solve the problem.

When cleaning in the office, disinfect all beverage machines and, if applicable, the cups provided to employees.

5. Keys, switches, and handles

When we leave our desk or office, other locations lend themselves to the proliferation of bacteria and germs.

Let's talk, for example, of the common areas where we find coffee machines, vending machines, microwaves, and water dispensers, all strictly equipped with buttons and/or handles and all in common use. Greater use by more people, therefore, implies a higher concentration of germs.

This is why it is important to contact a professional cleaning company, whose staff knows the less " obvious " areas to be cleaned completely and manages to sanitize the environment correctly, with the right servicess and a working method effective.

CHAPTER 4

ROOM BY ROOM CLEANING

How to clean your bathroom

Dirt, grime, and everyday wear and tear can cause the toilet to fall out. While it's easy to take five minutes each day and pick up your toilet, a deep bathroom cleaning guide can help you clean your bathroom and keep it that way for a longer period. We recommend that you take thirty minutes to an hour every two weeks to clean the bathrooms. Each bath, depending on the size, will take approximately thirty to forty-five minutes. You can alternate weeks if you have several bathrooms to clean. Keep a cleaning calendar in the cleaning closet to keep track of your cleaning schedule.

The bathroom

A deep toilet cleaning goes further by pouring some Ajax into the bowl. We still recommend that you start cleaning the toilet, then go to each area of the toilet. Use the same cleaner on the outside of the toilet that you use in the toilet or a cleaner from the same family. Mixing chemicals can be deadly, so be cautious. After cleaning the toilet bowl, seat, ring, and exterior, be sure to check the base and caulking where the toilet sticks to the floor. This area tends to mold and become germ because it can be difficult to see or reach.

Pro Tip: To prolong the effects of toilet cleaning, add a toilet bowl cleaner to your toilet. These cards are available in any large store.

The shower

Once or twice a month, scrub the shower with a basic shower or tub cleaner. If you have a glass door in the shower, attack those water build-up stains. If you wait too long, these deposits can become impossible to remove, so don't let them go too badly. Most of the showers have tile and tile has to grout. Grout can become dirty very quickly, especially in older homes. Clean the grout regularly, but if mold grows between cleaning sessions, take a cotton ball covered in bleach and leave it on the moldy spot for 4-8 hours.

Showerheads need love too. If you notice a drop in water pressure, there is likely to be a buildup in the showerhead. Take a quart-sized Ziploc vinegar bag and tie it around the showerhead for 12 hours. Then just remove the vinegar bag and start the shower.

We also recommend that you wash the shower curtain once or twice a month, and clean the shower curtain lining if you can't wash it in the machine. Plastic shower curtain liners need to be completely replaced once a year.

The Tub

Deep cleaning of the tank requires a light washing action. You may need to get down on your hands and knees to scrub the inside of the tub up and down. After cleaning the inside of the tub, use warm water to wash the chemicals down the drain and give it a day or two before taking a bath.

Wash the outside of the tub with an anti-germ cleaner and be sure to clean the putty that seals the tub on the bathroom floor. You can polish the drain and faucet with a little baking soda and lemon juice. It's also a good idea to pop the tub drains twice a month - it prevents buildup.

The floor

Wash all bathroom rugs while cleaning thoroughly and be sure to pay attention to the floor and baseboards. Sweep and wipe the bathroom floor and scrub anything that doesn't come off with a rag. Baseboards can be covered in dust and lint, so don't forget to clean them every time you clean them thoroughly. All floor surfaces and baseboard materials are different, so make sure you choose a safe cleaning method for your bathroom.

The walls and the door

While you may not need to hit them hard every time you clean, make sure your bathroom walls and door get a little recognition at least once every three to four months. Take a bucket of hot water with a light splash of dish soap and wash the walls. Do not try to clean the walls with flat paint with this method. After washing the walls, quickly wash the door as well. While it is not necessary to do more than treat the doors and walls every month, the door handle should be polished, washed, and disinfected weekly.

While enjoying your clean bathroom, consider renovating your bathroom or adding some extra pizazz to those freshly dusted bathroom shelves.

How To Clean The Kitchen Thoroughly

Every so often we have to give ourselves the time to thoroughly clean the rooms, one at a time. the kitchen is one of the rooms where we get dirty the most, and it requires more attention in cleaning. Because it is a place where we eat and our food can come into contact with dangerous germs, so now and then it must be cleaned thoroughly, to be able to live on an income, then cleaning every day after using the kitchen.

What we need to clean the kitchen well:

- cleaning servicess such as degreaser, disinfectant, etc ..;
- a basin, or an easily manageable bucket and fill it with hot water, we will use it to rinse the clothes and we will change the water often;

- microfiber cloths;
- silicone broom preferable to normal brooms because you collect more dirt or we simply use the vacuum cleaner;
- bucket and mop to wash on the floor.

How to start cleaning in the kitchen

- First of all, spend 10 minutes tidying up the room, putting in place what is in disorder: the more we can free the surfaces, the easier it will be to thoroughly clean the whole kitchen.
- Clean the table well and lift the chairs, to make space and keep the floors free.
- Start cleaning from the inside out, from top to bottom.

Clean the refrigerator

We put 2 sheets of newspaper on the work surface and empty the vegetable drawers and everything in the fridge. Throw away what is expired, badly stored, or any withered vegetables. Label the leftovers, don't throw everything away: let's keep them in airtight containers and write, on a piece of adhesive paper tape, the date we cooked them and put them in the fridge.

In this way, you will immediately see which trays to consume immediately, considering that it is always good to leave food in the fridge for more than two days. Wet the microfibre cloth in the basin of hot water and spray it with a sanitizer in the empty fridge. With the cloth, rub the encrusted and yellowed parts well, rinse the cloth several times if necessary.

With a new cloth, dry any residual moisture and then fill the fridge, following the instructions for better storage and arrangement of food based on the temperatures of the various compartments. We can wash the moving parts separately such as the drawers or the egg holder, wash them by hand or put them in the dishwasher.

Clean inside the cabinets

It's time to look at the expiration dates of flour and spices: throw away everything that has expired and put it in front of the packages that are expiring.

Clean the inside of the cabinets thoroughly with sanitizer and the microfibre cloth dipped in hot water. To avoid the formation of Camole (the butterflies that are formed from flour and pasta) put the flour in plastic kitchen bags and put bay leaves (well washed and dry) inside the rice cans and inside the bags.

Laurel will keep insects away and will give your pantry a pleasant scent.

Clean well under the sink and put all the servicess, sponges, etc. in order.

Clean over the cabinets

Before cleaning the hob and worktop, remove the dust and grease from the upper parts of the kitchen, so that the dirt falls and can be removed without fear of dirtying, where we have already cleaned.

Spray generously on the upper part of the furniture and rub well with the damp microfiber cloth.

Finally a trick: Spread some newspaper on the top of the furniture. in this way, the dust and dirt will not damage the furniture and next time it will be easier to clean, just remove the dirty newspapers and take them away, give it a quick wipe and cover with clean newspapers.

Wash the chandelier.

Finally, detach the curtains and put them in the washing machine so that before cleaning the floor they are ready to hang. Together with the curtains, we can also wash the chair cushions if they are machine washable.

clean the oven and microwave

Never use chemicals for these appliances as we risk breathing and ingesting harmful substances, which also remain on the food.

Put a container with water in the microwave and run it at maximum power for a couple of minutes, this will create steam and humidity in the microwave. And it will detach any food residues or encrustations. At this point, remove the container with water, spray the detergent and clean well with a damp microfibre cloth, rinsing it in the bucket of clean warm water. Wash the turntable separately by hand or in the dishwasher.

Do the same with the oven: turn it on at maximum temperature and put some ice cubes on the oven plate. Turn off and let the ice evaporate. At that point, spray the detergent and rub it well with the damp cloth. Wash the oven grill separately by hand or if you have a dishwasher, wash it there.

Once the microfibre has been used, if it is very dirty, put it in the washing machine and operate it once the cleaning is finished, adding the mop and any carpets.

Thoroughly clean and degrease the kitchen hood

Another part of the kitchen that is always very dirty is the hood, take it apart if it is removable.

Wash the moving parts, after having sprayed them well with the detergent with the damp microfiber cloth soaked in clean warm water, thoroughly clean all the parts, even in the corners.

Clean the hob and sink

Wash the grids and put them in the washing machine of the hob and degrease the rest well. Then dry with a dry cloth to remove any streaks. Let the services act for a couple of minutes on the sink and tap, and then remove it with the cloth in hot water.

If the kitchen sink gets clogged, can pour it into hot vinegar (a glass) and then let hot water flow at will for a minute, it will flow the pipes without damaging them and without causing problems to the environment. Then clean the cabinets and internal surfaces.

Other hidden kitchen cleanings:

- Doors and especially door with flap handle, the showcase of plates and glasses, even inside the showcases, accumulate dust over time. Wash dishes and glasses twice a year, the ones you never use.
- The feet of the chairs
- The lower part of the table
- The trivets
- The bottles of oil and vinegar
- The dustbin should be sprayed with the degreaser and cleaned deeply with the newspaper that will absorb any liquids, finally using bicarbonate to eliminate bad smells
- The broom and dustpan so as not to carry around the dust
- Plants, plants also need to be dusted.

Cleaning the floor

Use a vacuum cleaner or silicone broom and then use the mop on the floor, the microfiber mop that can be washed in the washing machine, and fill the bucket with hot water, together with the detergent and disinfectant. This deep cleaning of the kitchen will bear fruit and with a quick daily routine, you can keep it clean for many weeks.

How to clean the bedroom: practical tips

Cleaning the bedroom of the house is one of the routine tasks necessary to breathe and keep the environment healthy. Cleaning the mattress and pillows, dusting the furniture, sweeping the floor are interventions that are part of the basic hygiene rules to be respected to stay healthy and make sleep more pleasant.

Before starting the cleaning, you must have professional bedroom cleaning servicess, including detergents, microfiber cloths, a broom with an extendable handle, a vacuum cleaner, a steam tool. With this equipment, it is possible to carry out an adequate cleaning of the bedroom.

Air the bedroom

Before starting to clean the bed and the various furnishings in the room, you need to change the air. Therefore, opening the door or window is essential to promote air exchange and avoid the proliferation of germs and bacteria that cause allergies and seasonal ailments. Air the room for at least twenty minutes and then proceed with cleaning starting with the bed and mattress.

How to clean the mattress

Cleaning the mattress is essential to ensure not only a good sleep but to eliminate dead cells and bacteria that are constantly deposited there. To eliminate mites, steam is essential, the ideal solution to ensure maximum hygiene of the mattress. How to clean the mattress with steam? Here's how to proceed:

- Start cleaning by vacuuming all the dirt from the mattress
- Complete the cleaning with a steam vacuum cleaner to sanitize it
- Put a specific perfume services in the tank

In this way, every residue of dirt is eliminated and the mattress will be freed from annoying mites.

How to clean eco-leather headboard

Cleaning the eco-leather headboard requires special precautions to avoid damaging it. To keep the upholstery soft and bright, and to ensure a certain aesthetic effect in the room, first, you need to remove the dust carefully, then you need to use a specific detergent to treat the skin and remove any stains.

Using servicess suitable for the skin means safeguarding the faux leather headboard and keeping it unchanged for a long time. Like the headboard in eco-leather, the necessary precautions must also be taken to clean the fabric headboard.

The advice is to use also in this case a detergent without chemical solvents, specific for the fabric to be cleaned, to be applied with a soft microfibre cloth. Relying on professional servicess is always the best solution to avoid surprises and be sure to perform deep cleaning.

How to clean under the bed with a container

Effective cleaning under the bed with the container is a must to ensure maximum cleanliness and hygiene in the room. How to thoroughly clean the bedroom and especially under the bed with a container? A few simple operations are enough to remove dirt and sanitize under the bed. Here's how to proceed:

- First, lift the bed from the container
- Remove the bulk of the dust with an electrostatic cloth to be fixed to an extendable tool or a broom
- Vacuum the entire surface and reach the corners with the mouthpiece
- A small robot that can be slipped under the container bed
- After vacuuming all the dust, you can also wash the floor with a wrung cloth soaked in a professional services suitable for the material.

How to clean bed pillows

Cleaning the bedroom thoroughly also means taking care of cleaning the pillows. Taking into account that they should be changed every 2 years, you still need to wash them now and then to eliminate mites and bacteria. The washing changes according to the filling, and proceeds as follows:

- Goose down pillows - should be washed in cold water with mild detergent and left to dry in the open air.
- Latex pillows - must be hand-washed, rinsed carefully, and spread out of the sun
- Synthetic pillows - can be machine washed and spun without any problems

How to clean bedroom furniture

How to clean the bedroom well? For thorough cleaning, in addition to taking care of the bed, pillows, mattress, you also need to clean the furniture. First, remove all the objects from the bedside tables and dust them with an antistatic cloth that allows you to quickly capture the dust and does not spread it into the environment. Then wipe with a well-wrung microfibre cloth soaked in a specific detergent and finally dry with a dry cloth.

How to clean the closet

Cleaning the wardrobe is also one of the essential operations in the correct cleaning of the bedroom. To clean the interior, empty it of all clothes and proceed with cleaning using a suitable spray to remove dirt. Wipe the internal surfaces with a cloth and then repeat the operation to eliminate any residual dust. Then fill a bucket with water and perfumed detergent and wash the outside, using the ladder or a tool with an extendable handle. Finally dry and then proceed with the arrangement of clothes and accessories.

Clean the curtains

Curtains are also a receptacle for poor people, so when you decide to thoroughly clean the bedroom, don't forget to wash them. If they are made of synthetic fabric you can put them in the washing machine and use a delicate program or the one suitable for curtains that many washing machines have. Remember that they must not be centrifuged but spread "dripping" to dry in the open air, fixing them with clothespins on the edge so that they do not leave marks or creases. So, still not completely dry, you can hang them up again without the need for ironing!

Clean glass and mirrors

Window panes should be cleaned once a month to prevent dirt from accumulating and becoming more difficult to remove. Choose a cloudy day to dedicate yourself to cleaning the windows so that the halos that form when it's sunny will not remain. To clean the windows and mirrors you can use the same mixture: dilute 1 glass of white vinegar in 1 liter of water and then fill a spray bottle.

The newspaper is perfect for drying and thanks to the ink, leave your super-bright windows!

Cleaning the Living Room

The living room is a fundamental part of the house, the center of many activities that we carry out during the day and after dinner.

Precisely for this reason, it is easy for dirt and clutter to accumulate, making our moments of relaxation less pleasant than they could be. Maintaining order regularly is undoubtedly a good habit, but sometimes it also takes a deeper pass. So let's see how to clean the living room as effectively as possible.

How to clean the living room step by step

The longer it has been since the last general cleaning, the less we will feel inspired to get busy. The layer of dust on books and shelves, the stain on the carpet, the piles of objects in the most unexpected places ... all of which make cleaning seem much more demanding than it should. But don't worry: a little patience and the right disposition are enough to clean the living room in a short time and without too much effort.

To get into the mood, let's try to imagine the living room clean and welcoming, to have in mind what the final result will be.

How to clean the living room

If we have spent some time since the last arrangement it will not be difficult to find a curious variety of objects scattered in every corner of the room, many of which we do not know how they got there (clothes, books, games, containers, and much more). So let's start by gathering everything that is out of place, putting aside the things we want to get rid of (which we can eliminate directly).

What we want to keep can in turn be divided into two piles: the objects that must be in the living room and those that belong to other rooms in the house. We put the first ones aside so that they do not hinder cleaning, while the others can be placed directly in the respective rooms of the house.

Freed of all that was superfluous or out of place, the room seems less chaotic. Cleaning will now be much faster and easier.

Dusting and washing: here's how to clean the living room

As usual, everything becomes easier by following a precise method and steps. The first thing to do is to dust the walls and surfaces, keeping in mind the general rule of proceeding from top to bottom. So let's start from the ceiling and walls, using a broom or a vacuum cleaner (watch out for cobwebs in the corners!). We don't forget any structures hanging from the ceiling, such as fans or chandeliers.

Let's move on to sofas, cushions, and armchairs. In this case, a vacuum cleaner will be useful, ideal for removing crumbs, hair, dust, and lint from fabrics. The vacuum cleaner with the special adapter inserted will be equally effective.

When it comes to dusting shelves and bookcases, we can decide whether to take the opportunity to rearrange the arrangement of books, CDs, DVDs, ornaments, etc. In this case, we remove everything and dust off the empty shelves and then fill them again according to the order we prefer. Otherwise, just leave the items on the shelves and clean only the surfaces insight.

Now we apply a cleaning services to all the surfaces we have dusted, including tables, desks, television, and door. For windows, we use a window cleaner, while wooden surfaces require a special polish.

Tidy up and clean the floor

The time has come to give a first tidy up. Let's recover the objects set aside at the beginning and find a place for them on tables, desks, furniture, and shelves. We also arrange towels and pillows on the sofas.

All that remains is to wash the floor, but before doing so you need to take care of the carpets. We carefully vacuum all the carpets in the room, paying attention to any stains that can be treated with a special services.

We remove the carpets and remove the dust from the floor (and skirting boards), before washing it with a mop or a damp cloth. Let's not forget to open the windows to ventilate the room and allow the floor to dry faster. Once dried, all that remains is to put the carpets back in their place.

Following these steps we have seen how to clean the living room effectively, bearing in mind that each operation can be carried out with more or less care depending on how often we dedicate ourselves to cleaning the room. In any case, the environment will now be much more welcoming than before, ideal for some well-deserved relaxation at home!

CHAPTER 5

PEOPLE MOST EFFECTED BY THE LACK OF CLEANLINESS?

Anyone can get an infection, but some people are at greater risk than others.

Below is a brief description of some of the most vulnerable people:

PREGNANT WOMEN

At the start of pregnancy, the immune system weakens to prevent the body from rejecting the baby's embryo. At the same time, the body will have to meet, in addition to its needs, those of the child to guarantee its good development, which considerably tires the future mother.

This is why pregnant women, even in good health, must be vigilant to avoid contracting diseases which could have harmful repercussions on the development of her child.

During your pregnancy, just like what you eat, what you breathe can have a direct impact on the growth of the fetus. It is therefore important to favor a healthy environment. Take the right reflexes now!

Before airing the house, you must not smoke it. Let us recall here that nicotine crosses the placenta barrier to reach the bloodstream of the fetus, and that it is, therefore, advisable to stop smoking as soon as the pregnancy is announced.

Watch out for passive smoking

Have you ever given up on this bad habit, but unfortunately your partner has not made the same resolutions and continues to smoke? Inform him of the risks he makes you take: passive smoking remains the most frequent source of household pollution. Because the future mother who lives in a smoky atmosphere absorbs as much nicotine and carbon monoxide as a smoker. Passive smoking could lead to accidents during pregnancy (hemorrhages and placental abruption, premature births, etc.) and be the cause of intrauterine growth delays, alterations in the baby's respiratory, cardiac, and digestive functions. In short, ask your spouse to stop smoking! At least in your presence. Is your home "non-smoking"? Don't rejoice too quickly! In our overheated and poorly ventilated homes, the air quality is sometimes more toxic than that of the outside. It would be, according to studies, 2 to 100 times more polluted. And when we know that we spend nearly fourteen hours a day there, the emergency is in sanitation.

Air your house

To fight against the presence of volatile organic compounds (VOCs) which spread into the ambient air via cleaning servicess, heating, cooking, paints, etc., nothing is more effective than regular ventilation in his home. Open windows and doors wide, preferably at night before bed, or on a bright day. Even in the city, it is better to ventilate and renew the air than to maintain a closed and loaded atmosphere.

Above all, do not try to fight against possible bad smells. Room fragrances, deodorant sprays, electric diffusers are to be banned for nine months. They add pollution without removing it and you don't need it. Especially since, in general, nobody aerates after using them. Prefer orange blossom or lemon to chase away unpleasant odors.

Come back to grandmother's tips and recipes rather than succumbing to the many commercial offers!

Looking for a recipe? Dilute a teaspoon of baking soda in half a liter of hot water, add the juice of half a lemon, then spray in each room of your home using a spray bottle. Healthy, Safe, and Simple!

Safe to clean

Maintenance servicess are not harmless. If they are indeed clear, they leave traces with their users. How? 'Or' What? Remember that the future mother can be contaminated by pollutants in three ways.

While breathing: she can ingest pollutants present in the atmosphere which then lodge in her lungs and diffuse in her body.

By touching: contamination is possible by contact with toxic substances present in fruits and vegetables, for example, but also animals, furniture, walls, etc.

By eating or drinking: the harmful substance is then found directly in the body.

It is easy not to swallow anything. But it's hard not to touch anything, and impossible to stop breathing. It is therefore a question of taking some precautions. The first concern an activity well known to pregnant women, who always want everything to be clean: cleaning!

However, we have bad habits: to save time, we now clean. without ever rinsing. Wipes for the bathroom or the kitchen, non-rinsing detergent for the floor, hydro-alcoholic solution for the hands… All these servicess leave traces. Consequences: you breathe them in and are in contact with them for a long time to come. Not to mention the active substances, therefore toxic, of which they are composed.

"Nesting": info or poison?

It seems that future mothers suffer from OCD towards the end of pregnancy: that of cleaning everything before the baby arrives. They would scrub here, dust there, tidy up on the right, disinfect on the left. We then speak of the nesting instinct, of the verb "to nest", literally: "to build a nest". These irrepressible cravings do not present any real danger. But are exhausting, and often superfluous. Think about it before making your tiles.

Natural cleaning

In general, the mother-to-be should refrain from using chemicals to clean the nest. Again, a change of habits and a little common sense are best. Use ecological cleaning servicess for laundry, for example, and opt for disinfectant solutions as old as the world to drive away dirt: vinegar, baking soda, black soap or Marseille soap, lemon juice, etc. Besides their ecological interest, these servicess are economical.

Above all, rinse the cleaned surfaces with clear water: you will prevent the services used from stagnating on the furniture and/or spilling into the atmosphere. And wash your hands properly, that is, with soap and not gel. Last recommendation: when vacuuming, open the windows wide. Aeration always helps.

ELDERLY AND / OR SICK PEOPLE

Over time, the effectiveness of the immune system decreases. The human body produces fewer white blood cells, which protects it less against disease. This explains why the elderly are more sensitive. Sick people are more vulnerable to germs. This is especially true for chronic or serious illnesses such as diabetes, lung disease, cardiovascular disorders, cancer, besides in the following conditions:

- People who have recently been discharged from the hospital
- People whose immune system is weakened
- People who receive outpatient care

- People with an underlying disease

When caring for someone, you should create the best possible conditions for him or her to stay as healthy and comfortable as possible.

When you take care of someone at home

People who are recovering from surgery, illness, or receiving medical treatment are typically less able to fight infection with their immune systems. Hygiene-conscious behavior can protect these people from bacteria and diseases.

Regardless of the exact circumstances, there are many ways in which you can help a vulnerable person you care for lead a healthy and comfortable life:

- Cook the food thoroughly
- Regularly clean all surfaces that come into contact with food
- Keep cooked and raw food separately to avoid cross-contamination
- Make sure that food is boiling when reheated to remove bacteria
- Keep the bathroom and toilet hygienically clean. People who are not doing well are more likely to hold onto railings and handles than healthy people
- Hand washing is a must - for you, your patient, and all visitors.
- Keep the bed linen hygienically clean by washing it regularly on the boil cycle.
- Put laundry hygiene rinse aid into the rinse cycle to remove 99.9% of bacteria, special viruses, and fungi - for carefree, clean laundry even at low temperatures.

Home care for the elderly

Family members with acute infections such as diarrhea/vomiting diarrhea, wound, skin, or eye infections should pay particular attention to good hand hygiene. In particular, hands should be thoroughly washed or disinfected after using the toilet or after touching infected parts of the body. The infected people should not prepare food for other people. Separate towels are to be used for infected and non-infected family members.

In the case of bloodborne diseases such as hepatitis B / C or HIV, gloves should be worn if blood contact is likely. After removing the gloves, the hands must be disinfected. Surfaces contaminated with blood must be disinfected promptly and cleaned; gloves must be worn here. Toothbrushes, razors, or items that can easily be contaminated with blood must not be shared by family members.

There are many reasons why older people no longer take proper care of their hygiene. They may not be physically able to bathe or shower themselves, or they may have dementia or a mental disorder that prevents them.

When you have elderly relatives living with you, it can be difficult to address personal hygiene issues. How can you continue to be health-conscious without making older relatives (or yourself) uncomfortable?

Put yourself in their shoes. Understanding what your relatives think about personal hygiene and what their limitations are, will make it easier for you to compromise on daily personal hygiene levels.

If someone cannot take care of themselves, then help them with regular hygiene. Not only will you reduce the risk of infection, but you will also be doing a good part of that person's wellbeing.

BABIES AND YOUNG CHILDREN

At birth, a baby's immune system is not functioning, which makes it particularly vulnerable to infections. Of course, the immunization process begins very quickly (less than 48 hours after birth), but the progression is slow. It is therefore not protected against microbes.

Also, growing up, a baby's curiosity will encourage him to discover the world around him: he will want to see everything, touch everything, smell everything and taste everything. He won't hesitate to wallow on the living room carpet or lick the kitchen floor full of germs! Babies' curiosity and lack of "disgust" put them all the more at risk of infection.

For these reasons, babies and young children are at risk if the surrounding hygiene is not satisfactory. Without becoming an obsession, certain rules of cleanliness remain essential. Discover all our tips & advice for a healthy environment around the baby.

When caring for newborns / premature babies and infants, the following points must be observed in particular:

- Disposable diapers should be packed in a plastic bag and disposed of in the trash.
- Surfaces that may be contaminated with stool when changing diapers must be cleaned using a disinfectant.
- Reusable diapers should not be washed out in the kitchen; vessels should then be cleaned using a disinfectant.
- The laundry must be treated according to the rules of laundry hygiene and should preferably be washed as whites.

When babies and toddlers become mobile, they conquer their world bit by bit. Rolling, sliding, sealing, crawling - soon the floor at home will become an adventure playground. For parents, this means that a new level of safety and hygiene has been reached.

The topic of child safety in the home fills entire books. From stair guards and socket protection to rounded edges and window locks, parents can make their home a safe environment for their loved ones from the start with many useful servicess. When it comes to hygiene, however, opinions differ.

Floor & hygiene?

Parents often tend to declare their floor to be a sterile zone when their children start to conquer it as a play paradise. This is understandable, because the thought that the little ones slide their whole bodies over the floor, which the rest of the family walks over with their street shoes, makes bacterial nightmares come true.

However, experts agree: the floor does not have to be clinically clean for toddlers. A certain amount of harmless everyday bacteria is good for the little ones because it strengthens the immune system and helps them develop defenses.

So there is no need for long-term cleaning, especially not with aggressive chemical cleaning agents. However, certain basic hygiene is always indicated in a household with small children.

These practical tips can provide parents with guidance when it comes to turning the floor at home into a feel-good zone for toddlers:

Please leave street shoes outside

Street shoes experience a great deal. They walk along sidewalks, through public buildings, over parking lots, and through buses and trains. They collect all kinds of dirt and bacteria that are carried into the apartment in the evening. If a baby or toddler of crawling age lives in the household, the uninvited guests on the soles of the shoes are not welcome.

Children's shoes

Families can already take a big step towards crawling hygiene by strictly banning street shoes from access to living spaces. Perhaps there is a corner in the entrance area where street shoes can be banished as soon as they come in. If there are cozy slippers available for the whole family, your feet will stay nice and warm even in the cold season.

It is important, however, that all family members strictly adhere to the street shoe ban. Just quickly get the house key that was left on the kitchen counter? Under no circumstance! Even just a few steps can bring many unwanted germs and bacteria into the house. The ban on street shoes in living spaces should always apply to everyone. This creates a real feel-good atmosphere for the little ones in the house and the dirt-free zone is also noticeable when cleaning.

Regular vacuuming prevents dirt from building up

Much of the dirt that collects on floors in living spaces consist of dust, crumbs, and other tiny particles. Around 6.2 milligrams of dust per square meter are generated in households every day. Regular vacuuming, therefore, ensures basic floor hygiene.

In households with small children, the vacuum cleaner is swung almost every day. If a toddler is part of the family, that's a good thing, because little explorers love to put everything in their mouths that they find on the floor on their journey of discovery. Crumbs from breakfast, leftover biscuits from siblings, carpet fluff or balls of wool from four-legged family members, everything ends up in baby's mouth. Parents should be vigilant here and consistently vacuum up even the smallest dirt particles.

Children's carpet

Practical helpers can be modern vacuum cleaner robots that can independently remove dust and small dirt particles from individual areas of the home. When choosing a suitable vacuum cleaner robot, a comparison on the Internet can help.

So that the practical helpers in the household can also work properly, all obstacles should be cleared out of the way that the automatic suction aids would otherwise have to bypass. That means: put up chairs, floor lamps, and rubbish bins, roll up carpets and thus create as large an area as possible over which the robot vacuum can move.

Depending on the floor covering, a vacuum robot can also be used, which has a combined vacuum and mopping function. This means that the floors can also be wiped wet after vacuuming. To do this, it is necessary to replace the suction container with a water tank. The wet mopping function is only suitable for hard floors such as laminate, tiles, or parquet.

Attention: A vacuum robot must never be used unsupervised when there are children in the room, as otherwise there is an increased risk of injury.

Do not use chemicals with cleaning agents

In households with young children, harsh chemicals should never be used for cleaning. They contain substances that can irritate the skin, the respiratory tract, and mucous membranes. Chemical-based antibacterial cleaners also kill many harmless germs and bacteria that young children should come into contact with.

Families should use cleaning helpers who are as natural as possible. There are many natural-based cleaning agents on the market that clean particularly gently. But the tried and tested home remedies from grandmother's cleaning cupboard are also well suited. Vinegar and citric acid in the cleaning water clean thoroughly and at the same time gently and free of harmful substances. Citric acid is particularly useful against lime.

Raw sauerkraut works wonders against soiled carpets. Simply lay it on the carpet and work it in thoroughly. After a few minutes, the sauerkraut can be picked up again with a vacuum cleaner.

High-quality wooden floors can be gently cleaned with linseed oil. The linseed oil replaces every common wood polish and is also well tolerated by little explorers.

PETS AND HYGIENE

Pets (cats, dogs, guinea pigs, etc.) are an integral part of everyday life. They live in our homes and sometimes sleep in our beds.

However, the domestic animal can be the vector of numerous pathogens or allergens which can cause in humans more or less serious diseases. This is why the presence of an animal at home imposes some basic hygiene rules, applicable to the animal itself, to the people around it, and to the places where it lives.

Many people experience a significant improvement in their quality of life by keeping animals. There are pets in almost every second household in Germany. Pets can, however, be carriers of pathogens such as Salmonella and Campylobacter and cause allergic diseases (especially through cat secretions).

To prevent a possible risk of infection in the domestic environment with animals, certain hygiene measures must be observed:

- Pets should be properly vaccinated against diseases.
- They should be regularly monitored by veterinarians.
- It is important to ensure that the respective pet is fed a species-appropriate diet (e.g. prevention of dog tapeworm infestation; if possible, avoiding feeding raw meat, especially pork and poultry).
- They should not be kept and fed in the bedroom or children's room - especially for people with allergies - or in the kitchen.

- Your quarters and "toilets" should be cleaned daily.
- Pet care utensils should not be cleaned in the kitchen; cleaning utensils specially used for this purpose should be used.
- Feeding utensils and the area where the animals are being fed should be cleaned thoroughly and regularly.
- If disinfection is necessary (especially for sick animals), chemical disinfectants from the VAH list can be used.
- The contact of pets with food preparation surfaces is risky.
- Behaviors that encourage the transmission of infectious agents (such as licking the face) should be avoided.
- Hands should be washed after contact with animals, especially before eating.
- Body fluids from pets should be removed immediately and the surfaces cleaned with a disinfectant.

CHAPTER 6

WHY USE A "CLEANING COMPANY"?

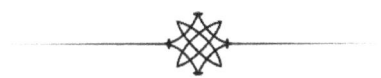

Generally speaking, you can contact a cleaning company at any time. Whether it is for cleaning offices, for disinfecting the premises, for cleaning after work on construction sites, or for cleaning roofs, the cleaning company is at your disposal at any time to perfect the area. Best of all, they can intervene at any time, during working days, weekends or holidays. You just have to contact them, make an appointment and that's it. A team will come to your home at the given time to do the cleaning.

What are the services offered by a cleaning company

Cleaning Company

In this period of the year, with the health emergency, there has been a significant increase in requests for cleaning services. Let's see together what are the services that are offered by a cleaning company, both in the private sector of homes or condominiums and in the workplace and environments dedicated to servicesion.

Housekeeping

Any private individual can turn to a cleaning company that takes care of the house, both for internal and external work. It is possible to request a personalized service and at certain times or for certain events. The services offered are different and range from cleaning and care of delicate surfaces to sanitizing rooms such as bathrooms and kitchens.

Besides, a cleaning company deals with: cleaning of glass and windows, cleaning services following a renovation, cleaning services following a move, pest control or rodent control service, sanitation service, interior cleaning (furniture, glass, floors, etc. ..) or outside (walls and walls, terraces, sidewalks, etc. ..). The cleaning service can be done on a daily or weekly basis.

It is always recommended to rely on well-recognized cleaning companies, having the full confidence that they clean with quality servicess and safe techniques.

The cleaning of the condominiums

Having a clean condominium is essential. One of the reasons for a dispute between condominiums often concerns cleaning. Sometimes the causes are represented by unpleasant smells caused for example by rubbish left in the hallway. In this case, a cleaning company offers the following services: cleaning of condominium stairs, treatment of delicate surfaces, environmental sanitation, sanitation service, pest control service, rodent control service.

All using specific and quality servicess to ensure the best hygiene and safety of the surrounding environment.

Industrial cleaning

These types of cleaning are often more complicated to carry out as they require specific characteristics with specific machinery and highly qualified personnel. The cleaning company must be very well prepared to meet the needs of the facility and with highly qualified personnel for a certain type of cleaning.

Let's see immediately the main services: floor cleaning, machinery cleaning, environmental sanitation, disinfestation, and rodent control, but also interior and exterior cleaning and green areas.

One of the main advantages is the improvement of the corporate image. Protecting customers' servicess will put the company in the best light and will allow for a stronger relationship of trust.

Another important thing to remember: the machines must be kept in optimal conditions, otherwise they risk not working as they should, therefore constant maintenance is recommended. Workers will also be positively affected: working in a clean and well-sanitized environment will allow a worker to work much better.

Cleaning and maintenance of green areas

This service requires very competent and professional staff who have specific equipment to allow the execution of certain jobs such as trimming. The main services are irrigation, grass cutting and eradication of weeds, tree pruning (carried out with the utmost care and based on the characteristics of the individual plant), regeneration of the turf, fertilization, phytoiatric treatment, felling, and clearing.

Maintenance is a very important factor if you want to keep the area in perfect condition. A well-tended garden is sure to make a good impression in the eyes of friends or clients. It is possible to call a company that deals with green areas even for a simple cutting down of a single tree that could have become dangerous.

10 good reasons to contact a cleaning company

Many people have already started using a cleaning service provider, this decision allows them to benefit from many advantages. Indeed, here we present 10 reasons to contact a cleaning company in the professional sector.

1. Good working conditions for employees

For a business, cleaning offices and other premises is essential. Indeed, the well-being of employees and therefore their work depends on it. They need to evolve in a pleasant and healthy working environment. Calling on a cleaning company is, therefore, an interesting option to improve everyone's working conditions and thus optimize results.

Indeed, who does not want to work in a spotless place where cleanliness is at the rendezvous? Just for optimal well-being, everyone wants it. For this, the best option will be to hire a cleaning company. The latter has the power to remove all the dirt as well as the dust in a room. This is so that you can work in an area that is both clean and comfortable. The best part is that these specialists can clean even the hardest to reach corners. In all cases, therefore, perfection is at the rendezvous.

2. Quality cleaning

Contacting a cleaning company is the best option to ensure the perfection of your home or office. As a professional in the field of cleaning, it has all the skills and knowledge to ensure the perfection of every surface. And this, whether it is a room, an office or computer equipment. Best of all, the teams of a cleaning company clean each area, following the rules related to hygiene and cleanliness.

Whatever type of surface you want to hand over to cleaning crews, you can rest assured that the risk of damage does not exist. To ensure the durability and performance of materials, cleaning experts use the best techniques and excellent cleaning methods.

Depending on the tasks to be accomplished in offices or other premises such as cleaning different floors, sanitary facilities or dusting computer equipment, etc.) They can clean any surface with precision, following the relative rules of hygiene and cleanliness and where the risk of damage is almost non-existent.

To preserve the durability of materials, professionals use effective techniques that are unique to themselves.

3. Respect for standards and rules.

The main goal is to avoid any health risk, whatever the type of company. So resorting to a cleaning company also means trusting experts who know the rules to be applied to the health safety of employees who will use the professional premises. It is essential, for example, if the company handles chemical or dangerous servicess certain missions are not within the reach of everyone, so care must be taken.

4. High-performance equipment included in the service

Cleaning companies have effective equipment and servicess that guarantee perfect cleanliness, which is why they are suitable for deep cleaning. They are thus able to clean all types of surfaces for impeccable cleanliness thanks to specific machines used by professionals but guaranteeing real results. The advantage is that industrial cleaning providers travel with their equipment, which is a serious advantage for companies because they do not need to deploy considerable material resources.

For small businesses, one can achieve significant savings over a year amounting to thousands of USD. Indeed, industrial cleaning companies have professional equipment and high-end servicess that allow them to do an irreproachable job. A company that has its cleaning team does not necessarily have the same materials as an expert service provider

5. Competitive price service

As we have seen, using a cleaning company initially saves money for small businesses. Besides, it is noted that the service charges of a cleaning agency are often more advantageous than hiring staff for the cleaning of the company. For larger companies, it is just as beneficial because the budget for cleaning services will not matter on the budget of the company. Indeed, the expert's service fees are often reasonable. This will not be the case if the latter hires household workers. The staff hired will be an additional burden, it is a huge investment for a company because it must also be attributed various social benefits.

6. Services tailored to personal & business needs

The frequency of cleaning and the surface area may vary from one company to another, especially depending on its size. The engaged cleaning company will be able to offer a tailor-made service, that is to say, a personalized, flexible and advantageous offer because its objective is to meet all the expectations of its customers. If you already have a person who can take care of the daily cleaning, you can contact the expert to carry out the one-off missions. Among other things, we can cite the elimination of storage space left by a move or an event organized within the professional premises. In other words, it is possible to access all types of requests.

7. Professional and satisfactory service

We must talk about the professionalism of professionals. They are discreet and experienced employees due to very specific training so as not to disturb the professionals of the company with whom they are in partnership. They come to the intervention sites with complete equipment. Also, by calling on a cleaning expert, you are sure to have an office that is always clean.

This kind of company puts a point in the spotlight in the management of human resources. Thus, in the event of the absence of one of its employees, it automatically sends a replacement. Initially so as not to disappoint your client and remain loyal to him, but also because that is part of their value, that is to say always wanting to be of service and do the best for their clients.

8. High availability

If a company wishes to move to other premises, for example, larger, and it has a deadline for the return of its premises. It can call on a cleaning company to make sure it can meet the deadline set by the lessor, in this way, the company can guarantee that everything will be ready on time.

You just have to contact the cleaning companies and make an appointment with them for the intervention, whatever the day they are always available to help you. The advantage lies in the fact that it allows each client to have work carried out when they want it.

9. Considerable time savings

Besides enjoying high-quality service, hiring a cleaning company also saves you invaluable time. By entrusting the cleaning to the interns, they must finish their tasks early and then embark on the quest for the cleanliness of the premises. This can decrease employee servicesivity and reduce a company's profit.

However, once you give the assignment to a third party, since this is often done outside working hours, it will not impact employee servicesivity. They can work at any time, without worrying about the cleanliness of the area. Besides, bringing in an expert also reduces expenses since you will no longer have to hire cleaning staff.

By delegating the maintenance part to a cleaning agency, the company saves considerable time. In particular in its human resources, where personnel management is already abundant and therefore avoids having to manage this personnel. Also, it avoids the whole recruitment of cleaning staff and follow-up of its files.

Then at the level of the maintenance itself, by calling on a specialized external service provider, the work will always be carried out faster and of better quality than if it is carried out by a person internal to the company of whom it is maybe not the main job. Especially since the material, it will use will be more suitable for deep cleaning.

10. For the prestige of the company

A company's reputation also results from the appearance of its headquarters, premises, and offices. Freshness and hygiene are major details that also reflect the image and brand values of a company. The company's professionalism and quality of service could take a serious hit if its premises are not properly maintained.

Also, the acceptance of new customers to its services then requires a healthy and correct image, therefore particularly in the upkeep of the premises, which must therefore be fairly regular.

CHAPTER 7

Business Plan

1. Frequently asked questions about the business plan

We want to simplify the creation of a business plan and lead you to step by step to a convincing business plan. We answer the most common questions that entrepreneurs keep asking us when they create a business plan.

What is a business plan?

A well- structured business plan is the back-bone and is crucial element for any business start-up. We will discuss each and every step in detail in individual chapters, for in-depth knowledge and training.

The business plan is the elaborated and structured summary of the business idea or the corporate concept. In the business plan, founders develop:

- Who the business idea is aimed at (target group)
- How the business idea should work (strategy)
- Where are the opportunities and risks (SWOT analysis)
- Whether the business idea is worthwhile at all (financial plan)
- This turns the business plan into a very personal guide for self-employment.

What do you need for a business plan?

Writing a business plan is only worthwhile once you have found a suitable business idea and examined important factors in the business model. For the business plan, you then need a stringent structure, e.g. B. contains the chapters founder, market, goals, marketing, and strategy. For a bankable business plan, founders then need a financial plan. A good business plan also requires time and a lot of detailed information. A consultant can help.

How much does a business plan cost?

A business plan initially only costs time. The business plan software entrepreneur hero can make free use of the business plan. When founders hire a consultant to support them, the fees usually range from 5,000 to 8,000 dollars. However, business start-ups only pay part of this themselves through funding programs. Sample business plans are often available for download free of charge or a low fee of USD 20-50.

Where can I find a business plan template?

There are many online sources for free templates for ready-made business plans. A ready-made outline that you can adjust as you wish and key questions will help with the creation. A sample business plan shows what the contents of the individual chapters can look like.

Why is the business plan so important?

The business plan essentially has the following 3 functions:

Check all relevant areas in a structured manner

Many things that are relevant to the success of your business idea must first be worked out. Who is the target group? How do you reach the target group? How are purchasing decisions influenced and who are my main competitors? Which location is ideal for me? Answers to these questions are compiled in a structured manner in the business plan.

Calculating profitability

When you create the business plan, you critically examine your business idea to check its practical feasibility (is my idea so realizable) and to check the profitability (is it worthwhile) of the business idea. This will reduce the economic risk of the project.

Guide to strategic and operational measures

If the idea is feasible and makes economic sense, it is time to implement it. The business plan helps here as an important guiding instrument. Ultimately, you decide on specific marketing measures, make important sales decisions, and set company development milestones when creating the business plan.

Do you write the business plan just for the bank?

Many start-ups say that they create a business plan because the bank, investors, or the employment agency want it to be. That is true and is also a valid reason why you should write a business plan. You create the business plan primarily for yourself because just as the business plan is an important decision-making document for external parties, it also helps you.

Who are the addressees of the business plan?

Business start-ups create the business plan primarily for themselves - after all, it is the central planning document for their own business. But several other stakeholders require founders to draw up a business plan:

Start-up grant - prepare the business plan for the employment office: If you want to make yourself independent from unemployment, the responsible employment office requires a business plan for applying for the start-up grant. The business plan must prove the sustainability of the concept.

Business plan for development and guarantee banks: If you want to receive subsidies from a development bank or a guarantee from a guarantee bank, you must create a business plan.

Business plan for the bank: The business plan, including the financial plan, also forms an essential basis for decision-making in the case of classic loans and financing from your house bank, as founders cannot yet provide reliable figures for their business activities. This makes the well-developed business plan all the more important.

Creating the business plan for investors: Even if it is often assumed that the business plan has lost its importance for investors and that other documents such as the pitch deck, the canvas, or the company presentation are the focus, the detailed examination is often about the more extensive business - and in particular the financial plan.

Business plan for business partners: It is possible that future business partners, would like to see a short form of the business plan, especially for newly founded companies.

What belongs in the business plan?

A bankable business plan is characterized by the following points, which must not be missing in the structure:

- Founder (team)
- Business idea & target customers
- Market & competition
- Strategy & Marketing
- Companies
- financial plan
- Opportunities & Risks

- Milestones & Executive Summary

How long should a business plan be?

One of the first questions that prospective company founders ask about the business plan is how long it has to be. The answer is: it depends. While 20 to 30 pages including a financial plan may be sufficient for a simple business model such as a shop or a restaurant, complex start-up projects, which are also linked to a large capital requirement, require significantly more content. Business plans with up to 100 pages are not uncommon. But the length is not the decisive criterion. The content matters when you create your business plan. And above all, that the founders adequately describe and explain all the important points.

Are there alternatives to the business plan?

The pitch deck, the company presentation, or the business model canvas are named as alternatives to the business plan. What all variants have in common is that they do not reach the level of detail of a business plan. Rather, the pitch deck or the company presentation show the central theme and present the highlights of the start-up project. They aim to arouse interest in financing among potential investors. They can undoubtedly impress more visually than the text-heavy business plan.

What is the difference between the Business Model Canvas?

The Business Model Canvas illuminates the crucial areas of the business model in more detail. This includes, for example, performance or services, target group, customer relationships, income, and expenses.

Due to the shape of the canvas, the presentation remains very superficial, and important aspects that are analyzed in the business plan are completely missing. So we see the canvas as a preliminary stage for the business plan. Develop a Business Model Canvas if you are still unsure about important factors in your business idea.

Should I create my business plan with Word and Excel?

Business plan creation using Word and Excel is certainly classic. However, both programs come with no special help for the founders. In other words, you start with a blank sheet of paper and you have to create an outline and all of the formattings for the business plan yourself. With Excel and the financial plan, things get even more complicated. Creating a financial plan with Excel takes a long time, especially for inexperienced founders, and is prone to errors.

Due to the mentioned problems of creating business plans using Word and Excel, many start-ups are looking for suitable templates with a table of contents and templates for the business plan, of which there are many on the Internet. Templates for the text part of the business plan in Word are usually not critical. However, the question always arises of who created the template and whether it corresponds to current practice. With Excel templates, in particular, the devil is often in the details. Are all formulas correct? Does the template fit my business model? The tool determines all key figures that are required by the bank, for example. And how do I integrate the Excel results into my Word document of the business plan?

What is the business plan for?

The goals, strategies, and measures are defined in the business plan. The financial plan is used to determine whether the project is also economically viable and how much capital is required. The business plan thus serves as the basis for discussions with banks and investors who are to finance the company.

Although practice shows that the planned development often does not take place as quickly, the business plan is important to set the framework for the project. It is an important guideline for entrepreneurial activity.

What are the advantages of a business plan?

The business plan records the central assumptions for the business project. With it, the target group is defined and financial estimates are checked for plausibility. The business plan thus later provides the basis for the reality check: which assumptions were correct and where should be adjusted.

Since there has been increasing discussion about the canvas and pitch deck models, the question has arisen again and again: Is the business plan still necessary? The fact is that without the business plan there is no money from the bank for founders. Many founders may confirm that you only have to write the business plan for the bank. First and foremost, the business plan is a document for the founder himself, as our 10 reasons and advantages for the business plan underline:

Advantages of the business plan

1. Less risk: the business plan is less likely to fail
2. The business plan provides orientation and structure
3. The idea is just the beginning - the business plan provides the details
4. Find the right market with the business plan
5. Analyze competitors and competitors in detail
6. The capital requirement is determined in the business plan
7. Business plan: Document for various contact points
8. The business plan shows measures that you will implement after the establishment
9. Success analysis and controlling through the business plan
10. The business plan is the basis for your success

2. Canvas and pitch deck as alternatives to the business plan

Are there alternatives to the business plan? The answer is yes and no. Possible alternatives are the Business Model Canvas (chapter 15) and the Pitch Deck (chapter 16). Both are shorter in size. The following table shows the comparison to the business plan:

	Business model canvas	Business plan	Pitch deck
For what?	Development of the business idea and the start-up project	Application for a start-up grant, financing by bank and investors	First contact with the investor
Addressee?	Founder or founding team	An employment agency, house bank, investor	investor
Scope?	Very short; Concept and key financial data formulated in bullet points	Elaborated in detail including a financial plan	Powerpoint presentation of 15 pages with a concept and key

64

			financial data
Crucial for financing?	No	Yes	The preliminary stage for sending the business plan

Result: Anyone who needs financing needs a business plan. The canvas is used to further develop the business idea. The pitch deck is the prerequisite for arousing the investor's interest in the start-up.

3. Content and structure of the business plan

In addition to the structure of the business plan, we have summarized the most important points for the business plan in an infographic. Take a look at the infographic before creating the business plan.

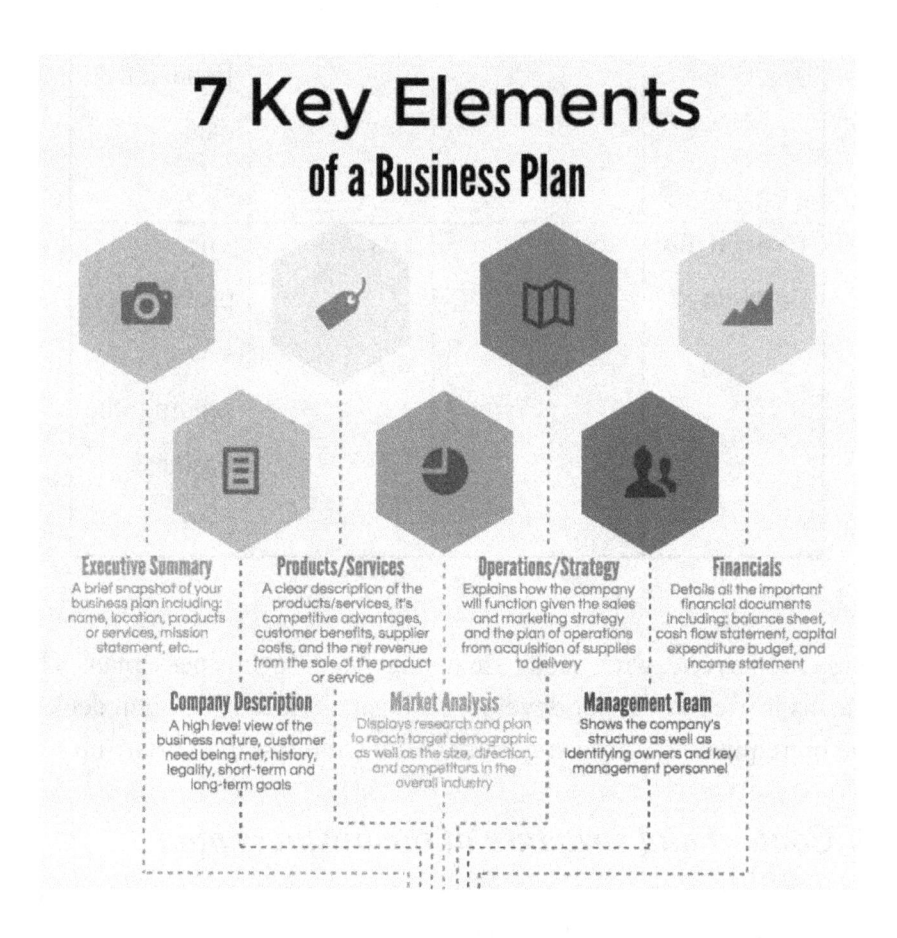

7 Key Elements of a Business Plan

Executive Summary
A brief snapshot of your business plan including: name, location, products or services, mission statement, etc...

Products/Services
A clear description of the products/services, it's competitive advantages, customer benefits, supplier costs, and the net revenue from the sale of the product or service

Operations/Strategy
Explains how the company will function given the sales and marketing strategy and the plan of operations from acquisition of supplies to delivery

Financials
Details all the important financial documents including: balance sheet, cash flow statement, capital expenditure budget, and income statement

Company Description
A high level view of the business nature, customer need being met, history, legality, short-term and long-term goals

Market Analysis
Displays research and plan to reach target demographic as well as the size, direction, and competitors in the overall industry

Management Team
Shows the company's structure as well as identifying owners and key management personnel

4. What belongs in the business plan?

The most important chapters for the business plan

We have shown you the main chapters for the business plan below. One-click takes you directly to the chapter for which you need support when you are currently drawing up the business plan.

Brief description of chapters

Chapter	Brief description
The idea, offer, and target group	The foundation of the foundation and the starting point in the business plan is the idea. In this chapter, you specify the offer and work out the target group. A precise definition of the target group then helps with the market analysis.
market and competition	How big is the market? How is the market volume developing? Who are the competitors and what are the possible hurdles to market entry? Also, carry out market research to convince in the chapter market and competition.
Set vision and goals	Where should the company develop? Set short, medium, and long term goals. These indicate the direction in which the strategy and operational measures are then coordinated. Also, develop a vision for the company.
strategy	The strategy in the business plan follows the goals. The question of which customer benefits you offer is particularly important. Position the offer in the market and work out differences to the competition. We present three strategies.
Marketing mix	Customers don't come to you! The magic word is marketing. But for founders and small companies, in particular, it is important to reach their target customers as efficiently as possible. In the

67

	Marketing chapter, you will also find a tool for the marketing budget.
Law & Taxation	Not exactly popular with founders, but still necessary for the business plan: the topics of law and taxes. From the choice of legal form You can find everything there at a glance, from permits, the company name to accounting.
Operational organization & founder (team)	At which location does the company start? How many employees do you need? What does the structure look like and which milestones are planned? As the founder, focus on yourself and show why you are perfect for the project.
Finances	The financial plan is the heart of the business plan: investments, income statement, or liquidity are the keywords. Determine the capital requirements and show how you intend to finance them. Our comprehensive tool helps when you create the financial plan in the business plan.
SWOT analysis	At the end of the business plan, the SWOT analysis is then pending. They summarize the strengths and weaknesses of the company, show the opportunities and risks and develop measures to benefit from opportunities and minimize risks.
Executive summary	Finally, in the executive summary, you summarize the essential contents of your business plan. The executive summary should not be

	underestimated when drawing up the business plan. Ultimately, many readers decide based on these two pages whether or not to read the entire business plan.

You should write the business plan yourself - after all, the business plan should also be as unique as your idea. Nevertheless, nothing speaks against downloading a ready-made business plan for your industry. In a finished business plan example for your branch, you will find important information, e.g. on the market and competition. A ready-made business plan is also suitable as a comparison document.

5. Advice and help for creating business plans

When you create the business plan, you can not only use our business plan software. You can also get further help and support for business plan preparation. We recommend the following 3 ways where you can also have a business plan drawn up :

Seminars and free consulting services: Seminars provide information on the basics of the business plan. Business start-up seminars for creating business plans are offered by the chambers of commerce, for example. The costs for seminars lasting several hours are rarely more than 100 USD. However, don't expect too much. After all, you are sitting in the seminar with several participants, which means that you cannot work on business plans individually. Due to the small number of hours, you touch many areas of the business plan. In the case of free advisory services offered by public institutions or the chambers of commerce and trade, there is the possibility of talking about individual contents of the business plan in the 1 to 2-hour appointments.

Supported advice from start-up coaches: The support from a start-up coach is much more extensive. The consultants specialize in drawing up business plans. The added value of the start-up advisors lies in their support with financing. Consultants know exactly what characterizes a bankable financial plan and what ideal preparation for the bank meeting looks like. The start-up consultation extends over 30 to 40 hours. Numerous funding programs cover a large part of the consulting costs and pay them as a grant. We support you in finding the right start-up coach.

Business plan competitions: Participants should create their business plan during the competition. There are also workshops, sometimes mentoring, information material, and business plan manuals. At the end of the day, the best business plans are awarded, and there is prize money and initial PR. Participation in the business plan competitions is free of charge. However, when creating a business plan, they are tied to the competition schedule and, as a rule, also have to use the templates. The respective business plan competition should match your start-up project. Find out which business plan competitions are available.

6. Avoid common mistakes and use tips

Over the years we have received many business plans from founders. We often noticed the following mistakes in the business plan:

Do not blindly adopt ready-made sample texts

Even if you should look at sample business plans for your industry, do not succumb to the risk of simply adopting this content. Every business plan is individual - just like your project.

Business plans are not written in a way that is appropriate for the target group

For a house bank, the presentation of liquidity is particularly crucial. The investor, on the other hand, is interested in the chance of a high return or a lucrative exit. So take into account the addressee of the business plan.

The focus is not on the founder of the founding team

Often the founders focus on the idea. But even a good idea is worthless without being implemented by the right person (s). What qualifications you have as a founder or your founding team is decisive. You should therefore give this representation sufficient space.

Market research is neglected

Are you convinced of your services? That is good, and it is even better when there are potential customers who you can inspire with your offer. Do a little market research in the business plan. This not only helps you to show that your idea meets a market need but also provides valuable feedback for services development.

"We have no competition"

Often in the chapter Market & Competition, you will find the statement that there is no significant competition. The alarm bells will then ring immediately for donors. So be thorough in your market research.

Customer acquisition: Advertising will do the trick

When you create the business plan, the first customers are still a long way off. And that's precisely why you should show as specifically as possible in the Marketing chapter how you can reach customers and, above all, what customer acquisition will cost.

Our services is great - unspecific customer benefits

Successful marketing is not only characterized by the efficient use of resources and the lowest possible costs per new customer. Rather, it is knitted around the clear customer benefit. Can the customer recognize the advantages of your offer, do they perceive them as advantages, and do they also honor them with their purchase decision? Often the customer benefit is too unspecific and the new offers do not have a successful market launch.

Financial planning too optimistic - capital requirements too low

Even with large companies that bring their servicess to market with a lot of money for advertising, it often takes longer before success is achieved. As a founder, it is much more difficult for you to assert yourself in the market. Nevertheless, many aspiring entrepreneurs are planning a very euphoric sales curve and the profit zone is quickly reached. Experience has shown, however, that it takes 12 to 18 months before break-even occurs. As a result, the actual capital requirement is often higher than originally planned and liquidity bottlenecks quickly arise.

Tips for a better business plan

Before you get started and create the business plan, take 5 minutes to read the tips on the respective start-up situation from which you are starting your own business. Depending on your situation, the prerequisites for starting your business and thus also for creating the business plan can be different:

- Make self-employment out of unemployment

- Starting a business from existing employment
- Business start-up from a university
-

If your clues to sideline own making

Below you will find practical tips that will help to make the business plan efficient, clear, and easy to read. For a convincing business plan, the content, layout, and language (not technical jargon!) Are particularly important.

Think of structure and design

Of course, the content-related topics such as business idea, market, marketing, and also the financial plan are the alpha and omega of your business plan. But in addition to the content, a business plan must also meet formal requirements so that it completely convinces the readers. A business plan with a clear structure, a convincing layout, individual design, and good readability also affect the reader's assessment. Keep this in mind when creating the business plan.

Use tools

Use tools to create a professional business plan:

- Business plan software
- Financial plan tool
- Price calculation & services positioning
- Marketing budget

Tips for layout and structure

An appealing layout helps the reader find their way around the business plan better. The following points are important in the business plan:

- Design a cover sheet.
- A table of contents for the business plan goes at the beginning of the document - the number of pages.
- The reader will also find the executive summary for the business plan before the details come.
- Use a fixed layout with a clear hierarchy of headings.
- Not too much text on one page. Use paragraphs and subheadings.

- The same text layers always have the same font size in the business plan.
- Use graphics and tables when creating the business plan - this is particularly useful in the Market chapter.

Achieve better readability

Make sure your business plan is written simply and understandably. Bad legibility is a typical business plan mistake. Some readers of your business plan, such as investors, are not specialists and may not understand technical terms. What to look for in the content:

Back updates with references.

- The appendix provides additional information.
- When creating the business plan, make sure that you use understandable language: write short sentences, technical terms should be explained.
- You will write the executive summary at the end after you have completed the remaining chapters.
- Finally, read the business plan from beginning to end and make sure that there are no contradictions in the text.

Preparation for investor talks

When you have created your business plan, you are ready for the first discussions with investors and/or banks:

- Before an important conversation, you should have the business plan binding and prepare it with other documents in an attractive folder.
- Know the details of your business plan so you don't have to look it up in conversations.
- Since the business plan is often very detailed, it makes sense for founders to create a company presentation afterward for discussions with investors.

7. Conclusion: What is important for a successful business plan

For many founders, it is a great challenge to write a business plan. Especially when banks and investors have to be convinced with the business plan. At the same time, there is usually a lot of time pressure as the founding date and the necessary financing are getting closer. Nevertheless, our most important tip is: create the business plan yourself! Don't buy a finished business plan and just swap names. This can be done quickly, but it is not promising.

The business plan is discussed a lot in the start-up world: do you need it or not? The business model canvas is highlighted as an alternative. Well-founded planning increases the chances of starting a business. Our recommendation is therefore very clear: write a business plan.

The business plan is more than a chore for banks, investors, or the employment agency. Of course, he helps to get funding for the start-up and business development. But first and foremost, it is your guide and very personal plan for business. It helps to structure the idea and the start-up project, to set goals, and to define measures to achieve these goals. Thus, it does not disappear in a drawer after the foundation but should be implemented consistently. This does not mean sticking rigidly to the business plan. Adjustments are necessary if framework conditions change or planned measures have turned out to be unsuccessful.

After the business plan is in place, it makes sense to create a company presentation. With 10 to 15 slides you can present your company briefly and concisely.

Business plan software offers many advantages

The easiest way to create a business plan is with business plan software, which offers you much more than a business plan template and a table of contents. So that you can make good progress with the planning of your business start-up. There are many business plan software in the market with which you can quickly and easily create your business plan. The advantages of such a digital template are obvious:

- You can start right away - the formatting and structure are already there
- Notes and key questions support you in the individual chapters
- You can also view a sample business plan free of charge
- You can use the invitation function to invite team members and create a business plan with them.
- At the push of a button, you can create a PDF of the business plan that you can print or send via email.
- If necessary, you can activate the finance plan module at a low cost and integrate the finance plan directly into the business plan.

By using many thousands of founders, the business plan software can be further developed through helpful feedback and is always up to date - unlike some templates that can be found on the Internet. Also, we developed the software in cooperation with start-up consultants, banks, and investors so that the business plan meets their requirements.

CHAPTER 8

THE BUSINESS MODEL CANVAS

Do you find creating a business plan to be intimidating? We have two alternatives for this. Business Model Canvas is the first one.

Your thoughts will certainly revolve around the various aspects of the idea such as the services, target customers, implementation, and much more. So that you don't lose track and a functioning business model emerges from all your ideas and thoughts, it is advisable to create a Business Model Canvas.

Find out below what exactly is behind this method. We clarify the most important facts in 10 questions. We also present you an infographic below for creating your business model canvas.

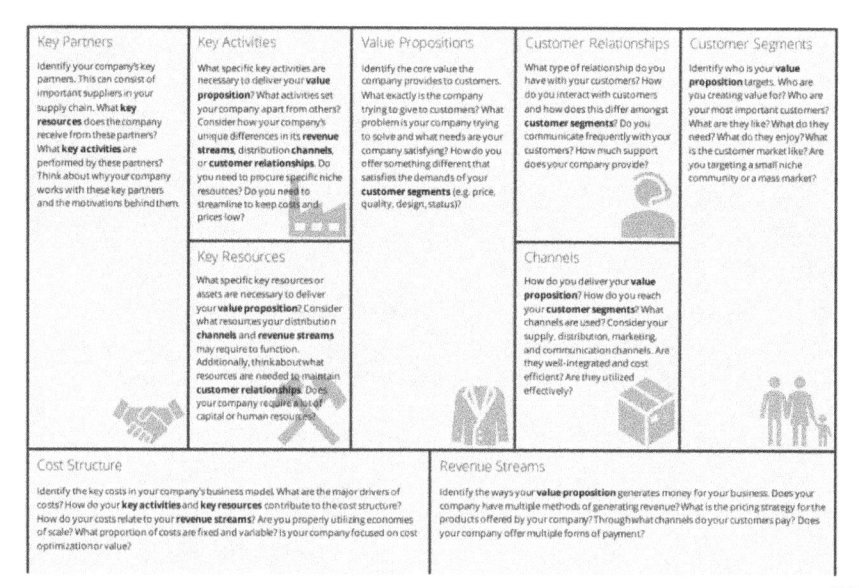

Key Partners	Key Activities	Value Propositions	Customer Relationships	Customer Segments
Identify your company's key partners. This can consist of important suppliers in your supply chain. What **key resources** does the company receive from these partners? What **key activities** are performed by these partners? Think about why your company works with these key partners and the motivations behind them.	What specific key activities are necessary to deliver your **value proposition**? What activities set your company apart from others? Consider how your company's unique differences in its **revenue streams**, distribution **channels**, or **customer relationships**. Do you need to procure specific niche resources? Do you need to streamline to keep costs and prices low?	Identify the core value the company provides to customers. What exactly is the company trying to give to customers? What problem is your company trying to solve and what needs are your company satisfying? How do you offer something different that satisfies the demands of your **customer segments** (e.g. price, quality, design, status)?	What type of relationship do you have with your customers? How do you interact with customers and how does this differ amongst **customer segments**? Do you communicate frequently with your customers? How much support does your company provide?	Identify who is your **value proposition** targets. Who are you creating value for? Who are your most important customers? What are they like? What do they need? What do they enjoy? What is the customer market like? Are you targeting a small niche community or a mass market?
	Key Resources		**Channels**	
	What specific key resources or assets are necessary to deliver your **value proposition**? Consider what resources your distribution **channels** and **revenue streams** may require to function. Additionally, think about what resources are needed to maintain **customer relationships**. Does your company require a lot of capital or human resources?		How do you deliver your **value proposition**? How do you reach your **customer segments**? What channels are used? Consider your supply, distribution, marketing, and communication channels. Are they well-integrated and cost efficient? Are they utilized effectively?	

Cost Structure	Revenue Streams
Identify the key costs in your company's business model. What are the major drivers of costs? How do your **key activities** and **key resources** contribute to the cost structure? How do your costs relate to your **revenue streams**? Are you properly utilizing economies of scale? What proportion of costs are fixed and variable? Is your company focused on cost optimization or value?	Identify the ways your **value proposition** generates money for your business. Does your company have multiple methods of generating revenue? What is the pricing strategy for the products offered by your company? Through what channels do your customers pay? Does your company offer multiple forms of payment?

82

The 10 most important questions about the business model canvas

1 what is a business model canvas?

A business model canvas is a method with which you can analyze your business idea and create structure.

2 why do you write a business model canvas?

By examining the business idea with a business model canvas, you can check the strengths and weaknesses of your business idea and find out whether the implementation is worthwhile from an economic point of view. Besides, you bring a clear line into the many thoughts that every entrepreneur has at the beginning of a business.

3 where does the business model canvas come from?

The Business Model Canvas was developed in 2008 by the Swiss entrepreneur and lecturer Alexander Osterwalder and has since established itself in various forms and designs.

4 Who is a Business Model Canvas suitable for?

A business model canvas is particularly suitable for developing or revising innovative and very complex business ideas. In general, the business model canvas is also very useful for smaller start-ups to get an overview of all relevant factors.

5 when do I write a business model canvas?

The creation of a business model canvas is particularly suitable for founders in the early start-up phase. The canvas can also be very helpful for entrepreneurs who want to further develop their business model or bring new servicess to market.

6 How do I create a Business Model Canvas?

You can easily create the Business Model Canvas using an online tool. Alternatively, you can use a large sheet of paper (e.g. A0 format) and write down thoughts on the individual areas with post-its. For this, you draw nine fields and sketch the answers to the key questions in bullet points in each field.

7 What exactly does a Business Model Canvas contain?

As a rule, nine sub-areas are described in more detail in a canvas using key questions:

- the services/service as well
- the related activities (e.g. material procurement and servicesion)
- resources
- Target groups)
- Customer relationship
- marketing
- Partners / cooperations
- Revenue as well
- expenditure

8 How long does it take to create?

With the help of online tools, you can create the business model canvas in less than an hour. Offline it usually takes a little longer.

9 how much does a business model canvas cost?

The creation of a business model canvas on paper or, for example, with our online solution is of course free of charge.

10 does a business model canvas replace the business plan?

We often hear that the canvas is suitable as a quick alternative to the business plan, as all the important sub-areas of the business plan are also briefly described there. However, we recommend that you use the Business Model Canvas not as an alternative, but as preparatory work for a detailed business plan. Because while a business model canvas creates structure and works out strengths and weaknesses, a business plan does more detailed work and can thus help to convince banks and investors. Read also the 10 reasons for a business plan.

Advantages and disadvantages of a business model canvas

The advantages of a business model canvas are obvious:

- It's easy, free, and quick to create.
- It does not require any training or the like but is intuitively understandable.
- The visualization makes connections directly visible.
- It can be easily created in a team and added to as required.
- It provides a perfect basis for the business plan.

These are certainly the reasons that have triggered a certain hype about the business model canvas. However, the disadvantages should not be ignored either. A business model canvas is greatly simplified compared to a business plan. It should therefore only be seen as preparatory work for the business plan and not as a replacement.

A comprehensive analysis of the founder of the team is not included in the classic canvas - which is one of the most important points of a successful start-up. Also, competition and financing are only considered to a limited extent in the canvas: Competitors, trends, and the wider environment should be presented in detail in a separate analysis or the business plan. The financial plan then forms the heart of the business plan. In the business model canvas, only incomes and exceptions are roughly outlined.

As described in question # 3, there are different formats and versions for the Business Model Canvas. The canvas contained therein includes, for example, a consideration of the founder (team).

The advantages of the digital solution are also the clarity and the simple possibility to adjust aspects at any time without great effort. Teamwork from different computers or even locations is also uncomplicated with the tool: You can use the invite function to invite your team members, friends, or consultants to work together on your business model canvas. Messages can be left via the comment function and viewed directly and clearly.

By the way: The business plan can also be easily written with the entrepreneur hero free of charge, digitally, and with valuable practical examples and key questions. When you have created your Business Model Canvas with the entrepreneurial hero, the first content can be used directly for the business plan.

Once you have created the Business Model Canvas and the profitability of your business model has emerged, the next step is to test your services (as a prototype). If this also leads to success, the next step is to write a complete business plan or to develop the business model as a preliminary stage to the business plan. This also includes information on the founder (team), the business idea, the customer, market & competition, etc.

CHAPTER 9

THE PERFECT PITCH DECK

Start-ups convince investors of their business idea with a pitch deck. For success, we show the correct structure of the slides and reveal which mistakes are to be avoided. So that start-ups can create a great pitch deck, we show free tools beyond PowerPoint.

1. Frequently asked questions about the pitch deck

What is a pitch deck?

The most important content from the business plan is compressed into a few slides in a pitch deck so that a venture capitalist receives an overview of the business idea and the financing requirements in the shortest possible time. The classic business plan is then often only required in the second step by the investor.

Why is a pitch deck so important to investors?

Investors are spoiled for choice and must be able to make an informed decision as to which start-up is the most promising and should receive the financing accordingly. Investors sometimes receive over 100 inquiries per month, which in turn have to be checked with a certain degree of care. Submissions in the form of a business plan are rarely helpful, as there is usually not enough time to review them completely.

How long is a pitch deck?

An ideal pitch deck should in no way fall short of 13 or 14 slides. There are pitch decks with more than 20 or even 30 pages from successful companies, but these are usually intended for renewed financing rounds when more context is desired.

When do I not need a pitch deck?

Founders and self-employed people looking for outside capital (such as a loan from the bank or a promotional loan) do not need a pitch deck.

What is the difference between a pitch and a pitch deck?

The term pitch refers to the presentation (with or without a pitch deck), while the pitch deck only refers to the slides that are used for support.

Do you always need a pitch deck for an elevator pitch?

No, especially in the case of very compressed events, where each start-up only has one minute available, you can do without a pitch deck. For pitches with a slightly larger time frame, pitch decks are often used.

Are there any tools you can use to build a pitch deck?

Yes! You can use conventional presentation software such as Powerpoint or Keynote to create your pitch, but the whole thing looks more professional if you use a special solution for pitch decks.

A pitch deck supports start-ups in presenting their business idea briefly and concisely. For example at pitching events where start-ups are looking for venture capital. Even angel investors often look at first the pitch deck of a company, before they request more detailed information.

A distinction should be made between the Pitch Deck and the Business Model Canvas, which in terms of content also partially overlaps the Pitch Deck, but is more suitable for the fundamental analysis of a business model.

TIP

The presentation of your pitch deck has to be 100% right from the start, so you should prepare well. For the creation and preparation, you can take the help of an experienced professional.

2. Content and structure

One of the most important rules when creating a presentation: the spice lies in brevity. A pitch deck should be between ten and 13 pages long. The slides must not be too text-heavy, instead of graphics often appear more meaningful. Try to tell the story behind your start-up in this tight space (storytelling) and arouse emotions.

The optimal film structure has emerged largely uniform through years of practice, but can differ slightly depending on the business model:

- Cover sheet
- Team / founder
- Problem
- Solution
- Services
- Market & marketing
- Unique selling point
- Competition
- Business model & forecast
- Proof of concept, testimonials & milestones
- Call to action/capital requirement
- Bonus slide: relation to the event

1. Cover sheet/introduction

In the introduction to the pitch deck, the start-up and the reason for the presentation are presented in a few words. Here it is important to remain as simple as possible. The contact details for the contact person should also be given on this slide. The core of the start-up should also be formulated in a concise, short sentence and well-presented.

2. Team/founder

This slide is one of the most important elements in the pitch deck and often receives too little attention from the founders. It describes the most important team members, their experience and know-how as well as their role in the company, in short: Who are you? And why are you and possibly your team, good entrepreneurs?

3rd problem

For every good idea, there is a problem that needs to be solved. The problem must be clearly described on this slide. Show how you can improve the current situation of the target group. Here it is also important to check whether this is also an actual problem, ideally as part of market analysis.

4th solution

In the next step, your services should be presented as the optimal solution for the problem described. However, not too many technical terms or technical details should be mentioned here.

5. Services

On this slide, the most important functions of the services can be described in more detail. A prototype or a demo in the form of a picture, website, or software can often be decisive for success.

6. Market & Marketing

Who is the target group? How big is the market and is it possibly already saturated? You should be able to answer these questions credibly on this slide of the pitch deck - here too, preferably with a serious market study or your market research. A brief insight into the marketing plan should also not be missing. How do you want to reach the elaborated target group? What is your conversion rate?

7. Unique selling point

Investors are reluctant to finance services ideas that are already on the market in the same form. Therefore, a clear unique selling point with the corresponding added value for the customer should be emphasized. Show how your services differs from the existing ones and what makes it superior.

8. Competition

Which companies in the market solve the same problem as your start-up? A list of the most important competitors and a description of the differentiating features is necessary here. The answer "We have no competition" is not accepted by any investor. Explain how you want to position yourself in the target market and what makes your services so attractive compared to the competition. The competition and your positioning can be displayed in a positioning cross. Besides, investors are faced with the question of how market shares are currently distributed and what proportion the start-up is aiming for in the next few years (assistance: calculate market share).

9. Business model & forecast

Ultimately, every start-up also has to earn its money. The business model is one of the most important slides. It should therefore be shown in a comprehensible manner how and from when sales are generated. If you have several ideas for sources of income, you should focus on the main sources of revenue.

10. Proof of Concept & Milestones

Venture capitalists are very cautious in Germany. The proof of concept, i.e. proof of concept of the business model, is therefore often a mandatory requirement for a successful pitch. This evidence can be provided, for example, by initial sales or the number of active users. Testimonials from any existing customers should also not be missing on this slide.

11. Call to Action / Capital Requirement

The pitch aims to convince the investor to provide money for the start-up. So it must now be specified in concrete terms which financial resources are needed, what they should be used for, and what can be achieved with them.

These eleven essential slides must not be missing in any pitch deck. Some investors also expect information on the market entry strategy, the status quo, and the long-term vision of a start-up. Depending on the relevance, the pitch deck can be expanded to include these slides or the most important information can be incorporated into the existing pages of the pitch deck.

3. Avoid mistakes in the pitch deck

The right structure is the basis for the success of your pitch deck. However, inexperienced founders can still make serious mistakes in the pitch deck, which should be avoided.

Too small font, too much text

Font size 28 looks large but is recommended for text. This way you don't get tempted to put too much text on one slide. The reader should be able to absorb the content of a slide within a few seconds. This is not possible with too many and too long explanations and lists. Ideally, there will be a maximum of three points on each slide. That's how much a reader can grasp quickly.

Bad foil design

The design does not have to be a work of art, but the font size and color, as well as the distances to each other, should be displayed uniformly. Despite all this, a presentation created individually by a professional is much more impressive than a standard design.

Missing corporate identity

The logo should be integrated on every slide and the colors, fonts, and designs should also be based on the corporate identity, otherwise, the pitching company will not be remembered. The big exception is the slide with the representation of the problem: here experts recommend not to integrate the logo under any circumstances and to use other colors in order not to subconsciously associate the services with the problem.

Animations and transitions

Moving images in presentations were popular at the beginning of the new millennium. Today animations - be it just the animated display of the text - are only annoying and should not be used in any pitch deck for investors.

No KPIs

Your audience wants to know what to invest in. Therefore, your pitch deck should contain all KPIs that are relevant for investors.

Spelling or grammatical errors

Anyone who messes up in such an important presentation may also do so in everyday business. At least one or the other investor will assume that with a pitch deck with errors.

Missing call to action

What should be achieved with the pitch deck? Many start-ups completely forget the CTA or do not dare to integrate it into the pitch deck. A pinch of courage helps here because investors want clear messages!

KISS & MOM

A simple tip to tweak the pitch deck is to use KISS and MOM.

KISS means nothing more than trying to make the pitch as short, simple, and straightforward as possible. All statements should be to the point, the pitch deck does not contain too many slides. The audience needs to understand your services or service easily. The easiest way to do this is to show your services or a prototype.

Another way to make sure the pitch isn't too complicated: the MOM test. Pitch your idea to the parents - or, if you are really brave, to the grandparents. Sounds absurd, but the reactions make it easy to see whether the pitch deck is too complicated.

4. Pitch deck templates, patterns, and tools

Templates and patterns for creating pitch decks are a dime a dozen online. However, if you want to create a professional and serious pitch deck, it is best to take a look at tools for designing presentations or especially for pitch decks, because there are useful templates - possibly with a predetermined structure or arrangement. PowerPoint pitch decks are also a popular choice for beginners.

Templates

There are many free pitch deck templates online. However, a free template has to be adapted to the corporate identity of the company; Finished templates can contain errors and should be checked.

Tools under the microscope

Pitch deck tools under a magnifying glass

There are numerous free and paid pitch deck tools available for startups.

Apple Keynote

The pitch deck templates from Apple Keynote were developed based on math and of course a lot of creativity. The interaction in the work process is a big plus: users can take documents or pictures with the iPhone, insert them immediately into Keynote and work with the team on the pitch deck from anywhere in the world.

Canva

Canva has perfected the drag and drop principle. It's one of the easiest and most intuitive tools for creating a pitch deck. High-quality graphics and the integrated stock photo database make the creation of a pitch deck a smooth process. Everything can be changed on request and with just a few clicks: font, colors, shapes, etc. Of course, it is also possible to upload your photos, GIFs, or videos and insert them into the templates. Some graphics and photos are chargeable as premium elements.

Google Slides

The search engine giant also makes presentations - and they are impressive. Google Slides provides plenty of free templates to get you started right away. Transitions can also be built into the templates. The whole thing only takes a few clicks and is easy and intuitive to use.

Microsoft PowerPoint

The classic among presentation tools. Pre-installed on every Windows computer, even beginners can put together a decent pitch deck. Working in a team is also possible.

6. Pitch deck ready - what now?

Once the pitch deck is ready, the search for investors begins. It can help if the start-up has already been networking. In the first step, the pitch deck is usually sent digitally (as a PDF) to an investor before the actual presentation. An appointment for the actual pitch will only be made after positive feedback. With this, it is then used again.

If you have no contact with investors, you can win business angels or VCs through pitching events.

7. Conclusion: present correctly

In addition to the content and the professional design of a pitch deck - whether created with smart templates or with PowerPoint - the way of presenting is of course important when presenting to investors.

Tell a story: Storytelling can arouse emotions and positively influence investors.

The first impression counts: those who captivate their audience in the first few seconds have a good chance of a positive overall impression of the investor.

Preparation is important: If you cannot explain how the sales figures in the pitch deck are generated, you have lost.

CHAPTER 10

BUSINESS IDEA, OFFER AND TARGET GROUP

You start the business plan with the basis of your business start-up - the business idea. When writing the business plan, make sure that you describe not only the business idea but also the target group of your business idea and the business potential. You should also try to emphasize the special features of your idea at this point.

Even when starting up with an already existing concept (franchise), start the business plan with the business idea.

Before the business plan: Check your business idea

Before starting the detailed business plan, we advise you to do a free business idea check with our business model canvas. Here you can check your idea for the most important factors and, if necessary, identify and compensate for weak points before the business plan. You can also use the tool to work on your business idea together with your partners, friends, and acquaintances.

The first step in the business plan: present the business idea

The business idea is the basis of your future independence and at the same time the starting point for the business plan. Based on the business idea, you develop a detailed range of services or servicess. In addition to a clear description of your business idea, which must also be understandable for non-specialist persons, you should describe the following aspects of the business idea in your business plan as precisely as possible:

Who is your business idea aimed at the target group?

No self-employment without customers! In the "Business Idea" section of your business plan, describe who should buy your services and what specific characteristics this target group has. You can also create fictional characters in the form of personas to visualize your target customers precisely and to get the most detailed picture possible of them.

In general, when creating target groups, a distinction is made between:

- Private customers (B2C) and
- Business customers (B2B)

It is important to know your target group as precisely as possible: What needs does it have? What buying behavior does she have? Who is it influenced by? When, where, and how often does the target group use a service or services?

What potential does your business idea have: business potential?

When starting your own business, your offer must meet demand. Describe in the business plan what kind of benefit ("why should someone prefer your offer over an existing one?") Your services offers to the target group you have defined and how great the overall demand could be. Ideally, you can also show how in the business plan how far your business idea differs from existing concepts and what additional benefits your business idea offers your target group.

Compare your business idea with an already existing concept (e.g. a franchise concept)! It may even be worthwhile for you to take over a franchise instead of developing a business idea yourself. You can find interesting franchise systems in our franchise exchange.

Even with a franchise: business idea in the business plan

With franchising, you take over an existing, usually already successful business idea. Even if the business idea has already been established, you should describe the concept as precisely as possible in your business plan and check whether the target group and business potential are also given in your case. Opening a pizza delivery service right next to Pizza Hut and Domino's Pizza, for example, should have only moderate potential, even if the concept worked elsewhere.

In your business plan, explain what makes the business idea so unique, who is behind the franchise (franchisor), how the franchising works in detail, and why this business idea will also work in your chosen location.

Not a good business idea? Your dream doesn't have to burst!

Even if you do not have your own or a suitable business idea, the dream of your own business does not have to be ticked off at this point. Let yourself be inspired or find out more about existing business ideas that are looking for a franchisor or successor.

Take over an existing business model as a franchisee

From Nordsee to Mrs. Sporty, from Studienkreis to Obi - many companies you know are franchisees. As a rule, they are constantly looking for founders who can set up new branches. In our franchise exchange, exciting franchise systems are presented with their ideas and are looking for new partners to start-up - maybe there is a suitable idea for you.

Take over an established business idea through a corporate succession

A company succession is also an option to set up your own business without having your business idea. Here you have the opportunity to acquire and continue an existing company. You will be active as an investor and as a managing director yourself. Thus, high start-up capital is usually a prerequisite for founding a successor.

Target group: Who will buy your offer?

Describe and specify the target group for your business idea. The central question is who should buy your offer - services or service - in the future. By delimiting the target group, it will be easier for you to record the size of the market later in the business plan. The direction of your marketing also depends on the definition of the target group.

In the first step, you can divide the target group into private customers (B2C) and business customers (companies, B2B). This is followed by a detailed definition of the target group.

Why define the target group?

When you have written down your business idea and thus the service and/or your services range, you should describe your target customers or target group. Your main question is: Who should buy your services?

If you know and have defined your target group, you will be able to address your target customers precisely. This not only saves you time but also prevents you from spending a lot of money on unnecessary advertising campaigns, for example. Ultimately, you will also be able to determine the size of the target group and thus calculate the market potential.

How to define your target group

No matter how great your services or service that you want to sell is - due to the different needs of people, you always only serve a part (segment) of the overall market.

The target group definition is about working out the characteristics of your target group. Characteristics such as gender, age, income, or place of residence are just as important as the question of what wishes, problems, or needs your target group has. Also, you can create personas in which you give your target customers a face and develop fictitious sample customers based on character traits.

Since the target group definition is not that easy, it is best to proceed step-by-step and first differentiate between the following two customer groups:

Target group private customers (consumers)

There are basically 82 million customers in Germany - the only question is which ones are suitable for your services. By defining your target group, you limit your potential buyers and can thus proceed in a targeted manner.

Target group companies (business customers)

If you want to address companies with your services, the industry or company size are usually important characteristics of your target group.

In the business plan, you describe your target group based on the respective criteria. Only in this way can you realistically assess the market and draw up sensible financial planning. The precise characterization of the target group will also help you later when creating the marketing concept and addressing customers.

Check the economic potential of your business idea

For economic potential, check whether your business idea has sufficient sales potential. You should first critically question your business idea and determine the customer benefits. With the help of the target group definition, you can quantify the size of your target group.

Once you have determined the buying frequency of your target group and the price that your target group is willing to pay, you can calculate the economic potential and thus the market volume.

Step 1: examine the business idea

First of all, you should check whether there is a market for your business idea. The well-known saying "where there is no services and no market" does not necessarily have to apply. You may also fill an interesting niche with your business idea. To test the potential of your business idea, describe your business idea using the following points:

What is your services or service?

- Describe your business idea in 3-5 short but concise sentences.
- Explain the benefits your business idea brings to the customer. What benefit does the buyer have if he decides on your offer?
- Present the unique selling point of your business idea!

You will describe the unique selling point in detail later in the business plan. Nevertheless, you should already find a few arguments why a customer should opt for your offer. The advantage of your business idea must be recognizable and significant for the customer.

When you have described the business idea, explained the customer benefits, and identified a unique selling point of your business idea, you can already assess whether your business idea has economic potential. In the second step, you determine exactly who you want to address with your business idea when defining target groups.

Step 2: Define the target group

Your offer must meet demand. The demand is determined by the possible number of buyers. You can find out how to determine this possible number of buyers for your business idea in the Target group section above. You can differentiate between:

Target group private customers and Target group business customers can be differentiated. The aim is to define your target audience as precisely as possible so that you can put the number of possible buyers in numbers. The target group size is the second of three factors to quantify the sales potential.

Step 3: the price is an important factor in the potential

When defining the target group, you have already determined which of the theoretical target group cannot afford your offer. What you still have to consider now, however, is the willingness to buy from those who could afford your offer but do not want to. Depending on the offer, this can be a limiting factor for the sales potential of your business idea.

It is therefore important that you determine the optimal price for your services. On the one hand, you should achieve a high margin, but you still have to be competitive enough and address a sufficiently large target group. If you put the three factors together, you can calculate the economic potential.

Result: the economic potential

If you have determined the effective target group, ie the people who can and would like to afford your services, and have determined the optimal price, all you need to determine the economic potential of your business idea is the purchase frequency.

With the purchase frequency, you determine how often your services is bought over a certain period - for example, your target group buys your services five times a week. Once you have determined the frequency of purchase, you can calculate the potential of your business idea.

Economic potential with a franchise concept

When setting up a franchise concept or as part of company succession, you should also work through the points mentioned above to be able to capture the sales potential of the business idea at hand as well as possible.

When you have calculated the potential, you can estimate how interesting a franchise concept is for starting your own business. Of course, the potential depends on various factors. For example, the location is very often an important factor for the retail trade, which can influence the economic potential.

Use the business idea check to assess the potential

Other important factors that can affect the potential of your business idea are best analyzed with the help of the business idea check. The free business idea check helps you to analyze the important areas of your business idea so that you can quantify the economic potential in a final step.

CHAPTER 11

MARKET ANALYSIS AND COMPETITION ANALYSIS

Based on the target group definition, the market analysis including competition analysis follows in the business plan. In the first step of the market analysis, you determine the relevant market size and deal with future market developments. With the help of the competition analysis, you can identify barriers to market entry, analyze your direct competitors and assess the attractiveness of the market. To finally determine the sales potential of your business concept, you can use our free sales potential tool.

For both areas, market analysis, and competition analysis, you can benefit from the sponsored start-up coaching.

Market analysis in 3 steps

Creating a meaningful market analysis is not that difficult. The basis is a precise description of the target group and well-founded market research. Building on this, you can analyze the market relevant to your business model in more detail and, in the last step, take a closer look at the relevant competitors.

1. Target group as the basis for market analysis

Since you have already defined the target group, it should be relatively easy for you to determine the market that is relevant to you. In any case, start the market analysis part of the business plan with a brief description of the market. Above all, this helps the reader to quickly get an idea of the environment, market, and competition of your business idea in the business plan.

2. Create a market analysis: how big is your market?

After you have explained in the business plan which market is relevant for your business idea, you can move on to market analysis. Unfortunately, one of the most common reasons why business start-ups fail is poor market analysis. It is all the more important that you shine here with a complete market analysis. Investors also value thorough market analysis.

The market analysis in the business plan begins with the determination of the current market size. Then work through the further chapters market dynamics and market potential step by step when you create your market analysis:

- Market size
- Market growth and market dynamics
- Market potential

Market size - how big is the market today?

The starting point of the market analysis is the market size. The key question here is turnover and, if applicable, units sold per year. The market size data should ideally be from the last quarter or year. With a current market size, you can also more easily determine the next relevant point on the topic of market analysis: market growth.

Market growth and market dynamics - what is the trend?

A complete market analysis not only includes the current status but also shows the growth rates of the last 3-5 years. A forecast for the market development (market dynamics) over the next 3-5 years is important for your sales planning and for possible investors, for whom a well-founded market analysis is crucial. Also, consider market dynamics if you want to do a complete market analysis.

Market potential - what is the maximum size of the market?

In any case, it is advisable to integrate the market potential into the market analysis. With the market potential, you answer the question of when a market is completely saturated - it is about the long-term growth potential in your target market. This part of the market analysis is particularly relevant for strategic planning.

When you have described and quantified the three essential points of quantitative market analysis, you should analyze further important, market-specific factors for the section market and competition.

You do this with the help of the competitive analysis, which corresponds to the qualitative element of the market analysis.

3. Competitive analysis: an attractive market?

Competitive analysis is an important part of market analysis. In the competitive analysis, you look at the individual factors that are important to a market. This part of the market analysis is not primarily about finding figures on the market size or calculating the potential, but rather analyzing and describing the most important characteristics of the market. The market shares of the most important competitors also belong in this analysis.

Michael E. Porter, Marketing Guru from America, designed the 5-Forces (5-Strengths) model, which is well known in the consulting industry, as part of the competition analysis.

The 5 factors of the competitive analysis include:

- Bargaining power of customers
- Bargaining power of suppliers
- Replacement services in the market and competition
- New competitors and barriers to market entry
- Competitors in the market

Bargaining power of customers: A competitive analysis begins with your customers and their bargaining power. How do customers react to price increases or decreases, how important is your service to your target group?

Bargaining power of suppliers: If there are only a limited number of possible suppliers, their bargaining power is usually high. You have to take this into account when analyzing the competition and think about how you can react to enormous price increases - especially if the customers in your market have great bargaining power.

Substitute services in the market and the competition: In the competition analysis, check whether there are alternatives for your offer. What new technological advances could mean that your service is suddenly no longer in demand?

New competitors and barriers to market entry: When a market is attractive, new competitors usually enter the market. When analyzing competition, it is important to determine how high the market entry barriers are for potential new competitors. Since barriers to market entry are also relevant for business start-ups, we have dedicated a separate section to this sub-topic of competition analysis in the market analysis chapter.

Competitors in the market: All of the above factors affect the market and competition and thus the rivalry among competitors. Therefore, a central part of your competitive analysis is to find information about your competitors and evaluate them. The aim is to find out how high the rivalry is, who dominates the market and which of your competitors are doing particularly well and why this is so. Since the subject of competitors is one of the most important factors in a complete competitive analysis.

The aim of a complete market analysis, which consists of the quantitative element of the market analysis and the qualitative factors of the competitive analysis, is to be able to show the strengths and weaknesses of the various stakeholders. This means that you can identify opportunities and risks based on the market analysis. These findings from the chapter on market and competition are valuable and important for the strategy, marketing, and risk parts of your business plan.

Market research: the basis of market analysis

If you want to create a well-founded market analysis and competition analysis, you will only succeed if you have enough information about your target market. You can find out where and how you can find numbers, data, and facts for your market analysis and competitive analysis under Market Research.

CHAPTER 12

MARKET SIZE AND VOLUME

At the beginning of the market analysis, the question of the current market size arises. The market size and in particular the market volume are important for the subsequent sales and thus sales estimate. Both values must be in a realistic relationship to market size and market volume.

First, describe your target market. After that, you can find out the market size and volume.

Determine market size and volume

As the first step of the market analysis, you determine the market size, which quantifies the turnover in your industry. The market volume describes the number of units sold. Both factors, market size, and market volume are important later in the sales planning and are therefore elementary areas of the business plan.

The size and volume of the market are also of great importance for potential investors, as this enables the attractiveness of the market to be better assessed. Take a step-by-step approach to determine market size and volume:

1. Market description

Similar to the target group analysis, start with the definition of your target market with the market size. You can describe the target market using the following factors and thus clearly limit it.

- **Business idea:** WHAT do you offer, what range of services do you have?
- **Sales area:** WHERE will you offer your services, which cities, regions or countries are relevant?
- **Target customer:** WHO will buy your service/service?

You have already defined the target customers under the target group, so you can simply adopt the target group definition.

Describe your target market as precisely as possible. The clearer the definition, the easier it will be for you to determine market size and market volume. A precise description also helps for the other areas of market analysis and the business plan.

2. Quantify the market size

Once you have described the target market, the next step is to determine the market size. The market size describes the turnover (in USD) that is generated in your target market in a certain period. Determining the market size is usually not that easy, so we recommend the following procedure:

Estimate market size using existing data

If you haven't found what you are looking for on industry tips, then you need to estimate the market size. Use existing data for guidance. You may not have sales figures for a particular federal state, but there is often information about the size of Germany's market. Using the available data, you can then estimate or calculate the market size.

Estimating Market Size for a New Market

If you can't find any relevant market size data, you need to estimate the market size. You can do this using the following formula:

Number of buyers * buying frequency * price = market size

Tip: Compare the result of your calculation of the market size with other comparable industries to verify your result for the market size.

Once you have determined the market size, you should also find it easier to determine the market size.

3. Determine the market volume

The market volume is particularly relevant for your sales planning. The market volume does not describe the sector's turnover (e.g. in USD), but the quantity sold. Based on the quantity sold - the market volume - you can then calculate the consumption per capita, which will help you, among other things, to draw up the financial plan. Often, figures on the market volume are already available.

Use a systematic approach if you can't find the right market volume data right away. You can divide the total market into individual segments and determine their market volume. In this way, you can systematically narrow down your market and determine the value for the relevant market volume. Based on the market volume, you then determine the market shares of the most important competitors.

CHAPTER 13

MARKET DYNAMICS

After you have determined the market size and volume, an assessment of the market development is due. Are you entering a growth market with your project or is stagnation more likely? Questions that are particularly important for your sales planning and investors.

You can make statements about market dynamics based on past market growth and other factors that you need to analyze.

Market growth: how has the market developed?

With the market size and volume, you have determined the current size of your target market. However, to be able to make statements about future market growth, the market dynamics, it is worth looking back into the past.

You can use the following factors for analysis to make a statement about future developments:

Market Growth Over the Past 3-5 Years

It is easier to gauge future market dynamics when you can show market growth over the past few years. It is best to take a look at Industry Tips to see if you can find market growth figures for your market.

Market growth due to volume growth?

The central question is how the market growth was composed. Is the market growth due to volume growth, i.e. an increasing sales volume?

Market growth through price increases?

Market growth does not necessarily have to be due to ever-larger sales volumes but can be due solely to price increases.

You can find price developments either in the price monitor or in the publication consumer prices (topic income and consumption) of the Federal Statistical Office.

Most of the past market growth is a mix of volume growth and price increases or decreases. Try to show past growth rates in your business plan. Ideally, you should show a graph that divides the average market growth per year into price increases and volume growth. If this is not possible, it is sufficient for the business plan to simply state the market growth per year.

Market growth can occur both through a higher volume (more is sold) and through an increase in prices (offers become more expensive). Try to find out what the main growth and contraction factors were.

Market dynamics: how will the market develop?

Since you now know the market growth of the past years, you can now make assumptions about the future market development, the market dynamics. The aim is to determine the market dynamics for the next 3-5 years.

Showing the market dynamics is important because it tends to be easier to be successful in a growing market. In a growing market, you not only have to compete for existing customers, but you can also acquire new customers who have not yet been courted by competitors.

The market dynamics also have a significant influence on your goals and thus the strategy of your company. Your business plan on the subject of market dynamics should contain the following points:

Market dynamics over the next 3-5 years

Give an outlook on what growth rates you expect for the next 3-5 years and what important trends could be that could have a positive or negative effect on the market dynamics. The development of the market shares of the competitors is also important.

Market dynamics: growth in sales volume?

Ideally, you can explain how you came up with the growth numbers described above. Are you assuming a high market dynamic due to a growing target group (more people can and want to afford your offer) and/or is the target group's buying frequency increasing?

Market dynamics: growth through price increases?

How do you see the price development in the next 3-5 years? How are the changes affecting market dynamics? Why do you assume an increase/decrease in prices?

It is important to explain in your business plan why you are expecting which future growth figures.

Market dynamics: The past growth figures should make it easier for you to estimate future developments.

CHAPTER 14

MARKET POTENTIAL

Based on the current market size and the assessment of market growth, the question of future market potential arises: what is the maximum size of the market? When is the market completely saturated?

Determining the market potential is an important part of the market analysis in your business plan. Trends and the services life cycle are important factors for the market potential. You can quickly and easily calculate the effective market potential and the resulting sales potential of your business idea with our free tool.

An important part of the market analysis: the market potential

After you have determined the current market size (including market volume), the market dynamics, and the market growth in your business plan, information on the theoretically possible market size, the market potential, is still missing. With the market potential, you complete the market analysis area in your business plan.

The market potential shows when it is possible to speak of complete market saturation. Statements on the market potential can provide information on whether the market will grow in the future (significant market potential available) or remain stable (market potential has been exhausted).

Your assessment of the market development influences the chances of success of your business start-up: because it tends to be easier to be successful in a market that has additional market potential and grows accordingly than in a market that is stagnating and whose market potential is low.

The market potential describes the maximum size that could be achieved in your market

The market potential describes the maximum size that could be achieved in your market. If, for example, 6 million wellness drinks are sold today, but theoretically up to 15 million could be sold, when one speaks of market saturation of 40% - there is still sufficient market potential.

3 steps: How to determine the market potential

To be able to make a well-founded estimate of the market potential, we recommend integrating the following three points into your business plan:

Trends in and around your target market

Existing or new trends can have a major influence on the market potential. It is important to recognize this early on.

Don't forget the services/service life cycle

The market potential in the growth phase differs significantly from the market potential in the maturity phase. In which phase of the services life cycle is your offer?

Market Potential: A Simple Calculation

After you have identified the market size, established market growth, analyzing trends, and determined the services life cycle, you can make an initial estimate of market potential. But you can also easily calculate the market potential ...

1. Trends influence the market potential

Describe in your business plan whether you are following a new trend with your company or whether you are entering an already established market. Mention the trends in the respective industry and explain in your business plan what influence these trends have on the market potential. A trend may also harm your market potential - that should also be part of the business plan!

You can find information on the trends either from industry associations, industry/market studies, or specialist journals.

Market potential

Example: Even if almost everyone owns at least one cell phone (total in Germany: 120 million cell phones), the market potential for smartphones does not seem to be exhausted: I-phones and co. Are likely to continue to gain market shares in the future.

2. Dependence on the services life cycle and market potential

When a new services comes onto the market, only small quantities are usually sold in the initial phase, but the market potential is also high. With increasing popularity, the demand and thus the profit also increases - until competitors recognize the interesting segment and offer competing servicess - the market potential decreases.

First of all, there is great market potential in the introductory phase. Following phase 1, the market is characterized by high market growth (growth phase) in which the market potential is increasingly exhausted. During the maturity phase, there is less and less additional market potential and the competition increases accordingly. The saturation phase is characterized by very low market potential, which then usually decreases continuously. In the degeneration phase, the services is then replaced by a new services, a new trend, as there is no longer any market potential.

In your business plan, you should indicate in which phase of the services life cycle you are with your offer. This enables you to better assess the market potential and you are already prepared for the next phase. The services life cycle is also important for future investors who tend to invest in a growth market with high market potential.

Market analysis phases

Example: The car phone was an absolute market novelty at the beginning of the nineties - there was enormous market potential. The market grew rapidly and brought the manufacturer high profits. With the cell phones, however, this invention was replaced relatively quickly by a new trend - the market potential suddenly no longer existed. Car phones became obsolete and the market collapsed relatively quickly.

3. Theoretically possible market size, the market potential

After you have analyzed the trends and defined the services life cycle, you can already make an initial estimate of the market potential. Nevertheless, it is helpful to quantify the market potential as this is an important part of your market analysis. You can determine the theoretical market potential relatively easily using the following formula:

Calculate market potential

When calculating the market potential, multiply the theoretically maximum possible number of buyers by the buying frequency and the price. The market potential is typically given in USD per year.

Market potential example - window cleaner

You have years of experience as a cleaner in a larger cleaning business and find that you do a better job than most of your colleagues. You are reliable, know the client, and believe that your own cleaning business can be at least as successful as your current employer. How to determine your market potential:

Target audience / volume

The following procedure will help you to determine the target group/volume: Question: Which customers would you like to address? Answer: Customers who want to contract spring cleaning services: In which area?

Answer: How many households are there in that particular area?

Answer: Approx. 50,000 apartments (possible number, the target group are therefore the owners of the apartments)

frequency

Question: How many houses in that area hire professional cleaning services for spring cleaning every year?

Answer: According to your experience, the apartments contract professional cleaning twice a year (frequency), ie around 5,000 apartments are professionally cleaned 2 times per year.

price

An average of 150 USD is spent per cleaning service contract (price)

Market potential

The market potential for painting in the field of professional cleaning work in the area is .75 million USD (5,000 * 1,50 USD)

CHAPTER 15

COMPETITIVE ANALYSIS AND COMPETITION ANALYSIS

The competition analysis is an important part of the market analysis. In addition to the bargaining power of customers and suppliers, you should also be aware of the dangers of substitute services/services and market entry barriers.

Identifying competitors and defining their respective strengths and weaknesses is part of competitor analysis, the most important area of competitive analysis. The competition analysis forms the basis for other topics in the business plan, such as strategy or marketing. Use our competition analysis tool for your competition analysis.

2 steps to the competition and competition analysis

The competition and competitor analysis are one of the chapters in the business plan that is read very carefully, especially by investors and capital providers. Ultimately, the question is what opportunities and risks arise due to the competitive situation.

Solid market analysis including market research forms the basis for a well-founded analysis. Another interesting question is which sales potential - derived from the competition analysis - can be determined for your business model. You can use our free sales potential tool for the calculation.

1. Analyze the competition

In the competitive analysis, you identify and analyze all relevant factors that could influence your target market. You should consider or examine the following factors/stakeholders in your competition analysis:

The state as regulator

The state can exert a significant influence on competition, for example by regulating prices and/or issuing permits. A component of your competition analysis should accordingly also be the examination of projects requiring approval.

The negotiating power of the suppliers

Describe the negotiating position of the suppliers in your market. In some branches, suppliers are strongly bound to their customers (eg by contract). In your competition analysis, you also show which difficulties your company could face due to a strong negotiating position of the suppliers and how you would react to them (this factor can also be relevant for the competition analysis).

The bargaining power of customers

Customers can have a major impact on pricing. Your competitive analysis should accordingly describe the bargaining power of your target customers. The bargaining power of the customers may also be important for your competition analysis, especially if there is strong customer loyalty.

Alternatives: Are there substitution services/services?

You have already analyzed the trends in your market under Market potential. Nevertheless, as part of the competition analysis, you should consider whether your services/service could be replaced by a new offer (substitution).

How high are possible barriers to market entry?

In your complete competition analysis (including competition analysis) you should mention the barriers to market entry, as this allows you to show which obstacles you (and possibly other competitors) have to overcome when entering the market.

The last and most important factor in the competitive analysis is competitive analysis. Because the attractiveness of the respective market and thus the likelihood of success for your business start-up depends largely on the rivalry between the competitors. It is therefore important that you also carefully examine the competition as part of complete competition analysis. In the next sections, we will show you how to carry out a competitor analysis.

In preparation for the competition analysis, you should determine the positioning of your direct competitors.

2. Competitor analysis: who are your competitors?

Competitive analysis is an important part of competitive analysis. In the competition analysis, the first step is to collect information about your competitors, which you should then process and evaluate. The results of your competition analysis (e.g. competitive advantages of the individual competitors etc.) are then particularly relevant for the corporate strategy.

The competition analysis is about getting to know the competitors better and being able to assess them. A good competition analysis not only provides information about the number and respective market shares of the competitors but also shows the strengths and weaknesses (which you can exploit) of the competitors. The competition analysis is also important for potential investors, who can better assess the probability of your company's success based on the competition analysis.

To get a good overview of the competitive situation, we advise you to approach your competition analysis step by step by answering the following questions:

Who are your competitors?

In the competitive analysis, you first determine the relevant competitors. It is important to know not only WHO you have as a competitor, but also WHERE they are active.

What market shares do the biggest, direct competitors have?

A complete competition analysis quantifies the total number of direct competitors and contains information on the market shares of the competitors. The aim is to identify the most influential competitors. If you cannot find any information on the market shares, try to estimate the market shares of the 3-5 largest competitors in your competition analysis.

What are the strengths and weaknesses of the competitors?

Finally, a competition analysis should also provide information about where your competitors have strengths and weaknesses. Strengths can mean insurmountable barriers to market entry, whereas you can exploit the weaknesses of your competitors. In your competition analysis, describe the competitive advantages and the unique selling points (or the special customer benefits) of the 3-5 largest direct competitors.

The most important findings of your competition analysis belong to the business plan. In the business plan, make sure that your competition analysis contains not only quantitative (ie number, market shares, etc.) but also qualitative (strengths/weaknesses analysis) statements about the competition.

Market research: Basis for the competition analysis

You have to obtain data, figures, and facts for your competitor analysis and competitor analysis yourself. You can use the following sources of information:

Federal gazette and company register: A look at the company register provides information on the financial data of your competitors.

Yellow Pages or the local: A complete competition analysis (including competition analysis) also provides information on the number of competitors. Use both portals to check how many competitors there are in the immediate vicinity. If, for example, there are already 5 cleaning companies within a radius of 100 meters, one can probably assume market saturation). You can also use the Google Maps tool for this by entering the competitors on your map (location-based competition analysis).

Direct competition analysis: If you already know your competitors, inquire on-site. Just drop by to check the range or offer for your competitor analysis!

Competitor analysis with the help of the competitor analysis tool

The aim of the competition and competitor analysis is ...... that in this section of the business plan you explain exactly who your main competitors are, what they do well or less well, and how competitive the market is. After the competition and competition analysis, you and the reader (e.g. investor or bank) should be able to roughly estimate your chances of success for entering the market.

With the competition analysis and the competition analysis, you close the "market" area in your business plan with the market entry barriers.

After that, it is a matter of setting realistic company goals in the market that you now know.

CHAPTER 16

MARKET SHARE: METHODS AND FORMULAS

The market share describes the market power of a company. The calculation of the market share helps to determine the position of one's own company in the market, to assess the development of the business, and to check the results of marketing strategies. We show how the calculation of the market share for the market and competition analysis succeeds.

1. What does market share mean?

The market share describes what shares a company has in the market: either in terms of volume (based on sales) or in terms of value (based on sales). It should be noted that the market share is constantly changing. For meaningful results, a single, specific period for which the market share is calculated: for example, the market share in the previous year or the planned market share in the next year.

Usually, the market share is calculated as a percentage. To determine the market share, the so-called "relevant market" must first be determined. For example, a window cleaner company competes with other window cleaning company in the same class and not in the overall cleaning market.

Absolute and relative market share: what is the difference?

There are two ways to look at market share:

Absolute market share

A calculation of the absolute market share shows how large the turnover or sales share of the respective company is concerning the total market volume of the industry.

It makes sense to calculate the absolute market share to get an overview of the market:

How is it structured?

Are only a handful of large companies competing ("oligopoly market")?

Does the market consist of many small companies ("populistic market")?

These considerations help to better assess the chances of your own company and are an important part of the competitive analysis in the business plan.

Relative market share

The calculation of the relative market share shows the share of a company compared to the market share of the largest competitor. The relative market share can be used to calculate who is the market leader and what the ratio is among the competitors. If you have calculated a relative market share of more than 100% for your own company, you are the market leader. Then it is necessary to check which advantages (e.g. concerning image, services/serviceion costs, etc.) result from this and whether the economies of scale can be further exploited. If you have calculated a relative market share of less than 100%, the next step is to check how much the competitor is stronger and what disadvantages this results for your company. They think,

2. Calculate market share: method, and formula

You determine the market share in two steps:

- Determination of the market volume or the market potential of the relevant market
- Determination of the sales of the 3 to 5 most important competitors

How big is the relevant market?

Only the relevant market counts for the market share calculation. It is the market that a company can theoretically reach. Entrepreneurs use official sources as sources for market research, for example from the Federal Statistical Office. Banks, professional chambers, the IHK, and industry associations and banks often publish turnover and sales figures for certain industries. If the market is regionally limited, qualitative estimation is the order of the day. One method is to determine the number of providers and estimate their sales.

You can also segment the relevant market of the industry according to the target group, region, or specific services/service groups. At the end of the analysis, you have an approximate estimate of the market volume or the market size of the relevant market.

A question of positioning

The relevant market is also a question of positioning. For example a company cleaning service should be positioned somewhere near the commercial area, having lots of companies and offices.

What is the turnover of the competitors?

Finding this number is more difficult. Because no competitor voluntarily reveals its business figures. The principle of qualitative estimation also applies here.

Formula: Absolute market share

You can calculate the absolute market share using the formula:

Own sales / total market sales x 100

Here is an example calculation: Your company has a total turnover of 5 million USD. The relevant overall market achieved a turnover of 200 million USD. This results in the following calculation: 5 million: 200 million x 100 = 2.5. This means that your own company's market share is 2.5%.

Formula: Relative market share

The formula for the relative market share is the same, but the calculation is not based on total sales or sales, but rather on sales of the strongest competitor. So:

Own sales of the strongest competitor x 100

Example: Your company again achieved a total turnover of 5 million USD. The strongest competitor has a turnover of 40 million USD. The calculation of the relative market share: 5 million: 40 million x 100 = 12.5. Their relative market share is 12.5%.

Why calculate market share?

The calculation of the market share allows an assessment of one's position on the market. The key figure "market share" clearly shows the position of your company in the competition. From this, market opportunities can be derived, marketing strategies can be developed and marketing measures carried out can be assessed retrospectively. The market share is therefore an important basis for marketing plans and future corporate strategies.

It is also worth calculating the market share for a comparison with the competition. The following considerations result, for example:

- Who is the biggest competitor?
- What are the competitive advantages of the size?
- Are there any cost advantages or other advantages?

Is it possible to attack the market leader directly or is it worth looking at an interesting niche?

Last but not least, the calculation of the market share provides information about the nature of the market, for example, whether it is a monopoly (1 single supplier), an oligopoly (several large suppliers), or a polyol (many small suppliers).

3. *Common questions about market share*

Why is market share important?

With the market share, the entrepreneur calculates the share of his company in the market. This provides information on your position in the competition, on opportunities and risks. Besides, the entrepreneur can better assess his competitive advantages and those of the competition.

What does a high market share bring?

A high market share can bring the following potentials and competitive advantages:

Cost advantages through size

Marketing advantages through awareness, image, and access to advertising channels that are closed to smaller competitors.

Large companies may find it easier to find staff because everyone enjoys working for the winner.

What disadvantages can a high market share have?

- The bigger the market share, the bigger the company. Size can lead to disadvantages such as:
- bureaucracy
- Difficult decisions
- Customer proximity is lost

Does a founder have to strive for the largest market share?

Not necessarily if the behavior of competitors is such that every market participant makes a good living. Or when there are profitable niches.

What should never be forgotten when looking at market share?

When setting up and developing a company, it is certainly important to pay attention to service quality and customer proximity.

Is a low market share generally bad?

No, otherwise nobody would start a business anymore. Because when the company is founded, the founder's market share is logically 0%. If an entrepreneur finds the right niche, a profitable business model can result for him.

How is the relevant market determined?

There are different ways of determining the relevant market. It can, for example, depend on the services/service itself (e.g. new soft drink), but it can also be determined in terms of time (e.g. for seasonal services/services) or location (for regional offers). The relevant market can also be narrowed down based on the target group.

Why should entrepreneurs calculate the market share of their competitors?

By calculating the absolute market share of other competitors, you get an overview of the structure of the market. This enables you to better assess what chances you have of asserting yourself against competitors with your company.

What role does market share play in antitrust law?

The market share also shows whether there is a so-called "dominant position" - then the rules of antitrust law that you as an entrepreneur must comply with applying. It is therefore important that you calculate your market share if you suspect such a dominant position. This is assumed from an absolute market share of 40% but can be refuted. From a share of 50%, the dominant position is clear. Companies in this position must, among other things, avoid "improper abuse" of this special position. This can include, for example, certain pricing mechanisms or the design of terms and conditions.

4. Conclusion

Market share enables entrepreneurs to assess the company's current success and future competitive prospects. The key figure is closely related to the market and competition analysis, which should also be anchored in the business plan. The calculation is quite simple using a formula once the data on the market volume is available. In addition to calculating the market share, estimating market growth and market potential are important for a successful start-up. Are you having trouble calculating? Then use targeted start-up coaching and get competent help by your side.

CHAPTER 17

COMPANY GOALS AND OBJECTIVES

The company goals in the business plan follow the market analysis. First, formulate the long-term company goals, vision, and mission. After that, you can set the short and medium-term business goals. Based on the short and medium-term company goals, you determine milestones for the next 1-3 years, which you will use as a guide for your company's development.

Based on the business goals set in the business, plan the company strategy firmly.

Set corporate goals: where do you want to go?

The quote from Mark Twain "If you don't know where you want to go, you shouldn't be surprised when you get somewhere else" aptly describes why you should define clear corporate goals for your company. As an entrepreneur, you need to know where to go or want to stand with your company for 3 or 10 years.

Since corporate goals also depend on the respective market development, the chapter corporate goals in the business plan always follow the market analysis. Based on the current market size and market growth, it will be much easier for you to define realistic company goals.

Before you start setting business goals, however, you should take a step back and ask yourself what your intentions are in starting your business. If you intend to secure your livelihood with the project (proper business start-up), the conditions are completely different than if, for example, you see an additional source of income in your project (step-by-step business start-up?) Or it may not be about making a profit at all. Make a note of this point in your business plan, as it is relevant for the other parts of the business plan and especially for the corporate goals.

The corporate goals then follow the intentions. It is best to start by defining the long-term corporate goals (mission and vision) and then determine the medium and short-term corporate goals step by step. Then you can set the milestones with which you want to achieve the company goals.

Corporate goals

Company goals: The vision is followed by medium and short-term company goals and milestones.

Long-term corporate goals: Vision & Mission

With the vision, you describe the ideal state of your company in the distant future and thus answer the question of what you would like to achieve with your company in the long term (i.e. in 10 to 25 years). The vision is therefore an overarching corporate goal.

When formulating the vision in your business plan, make sure that the vision:

- "Visionary" but still realistic,
- is clearly and understandably formulated and
- can be expressed in one sentence (focusing on the essential factors).

In contrast to the vision, with which your employees, in particular, should identify, the mission is aimed to explain the purpose of the company. Essentially, it is about what a company should do for customers and/or society or what purpose the company should fulfill. The mission is usually derived from the vision and accordingly has an indirect impact on the corporate goals.

Take the two long-term corporate goals, vision and mission, into your business plan. Based on this, you can then set the short and medium-term corporate goals and milestones.

Short and medium-term corporate goals

When you have formulated the vision and mission, it is a matter of defining the medium to long-term company goals (for the next 5-10 years) as well as the short-term company goals (1-3 years). Based on the short-term company goals, you can then define the milestones that you can use as a guide when implementing the business plan.

CHAPTER 19

CORPORATE STRATEGY: HOW TO ACHIEVE YOUR GOALS

With the corporate goals, you have determined which milestones you would like to have reached by WHEN. With the corporate strategy, you show in the business plan HOW you want to achieve these goals. One of the 3 corporate strategies comes into question: cost leadership, differentiation, or niche strategy.

The starting point for the corporate strategy is the customer benefit of your offer and the positioning of your company in the market.

The corporate strategy follows goals

After you have set the company goals and milestones, you now have to answer the question of how you want to achieve these goals.

The corporate strategy in your business plan provides answers and shows the path that should ultimately lead to the achievement of goals.

The starting point for a successful corporate strategy is always a complete market analysis. Determining the market growth and the market potential is just as important as a comprehensive competition analysis.

Based on the findings, you can determine the comparative competitive advantage that puts your offer concerning the other offers and then determines the positioning. Based on the positioning, it is then relatively easy to find the right corporate strategy.

The corporate strategy shows how you want to achieve your corporate goals.

1. Basis of the corporate strategy: the customer benefit

If you do not offer any particular customer benefit (competitive advantage), it will be very difficult to remain successful in the long term. The special customer benefits can appear in the most varied of forms (price, quality, service, etc.).

Since the special customer benefit (also known as USP; Unique Selling Proposition or USP) is an important part of a corporate strategy.

2. Basis of the corporate strategy: the positioning

A clear positioning is essential for a successful start-up. With the positioning, you determine where you want to stand in comparison to the competition in terms of price-performance ratio. The positioning not only helps to find the right corporate strategy but also clearly signals to the customer in which segment the customer can place your offer. The positioning depends heavily on the particular customer benefit and accordingly follows the customer benefit in the business plan.

The heart: the right corporate strategy

When you have worked through the, Customer Value and Positioning in the Business Plan, it should be relatively easy to determine the right corporate strategy for your company.

When it comes to corporate strategy, it is best to proceed in two steps:

Determine

the right corporate strategy In addition to the niche corporate strategy (very clearly defined, specialized, and mostly small market), you can either establish yourself as a cost leader or differentiate yourself from competitors with the corporate strategy differentiation.

Determine the alignment of the corporate strategy to whom you align the corporate strategy essentially depends on the marketing strategy.

Which corporate strategy you ultimately decide on depends, among other things, on your business model.

It is particularly important that you consider a defined corporate strategy in the other areas of the business plan (in particular marketing & organization) and then implement the corporate strategy consistently.

Corporate strategy: cost leader, differentiation, or niche? Determine the corporate strategy for your start-up.

The goal is ...... that you make it clear in your business plan why you have chosen which corporate strategy. The customer benefit, the special competitive advantage, and the positioning are important factors influencing the determination of the corporate strategy.

The corporate strategy forms the basis for many parts of your business model in the business plan (e.g. cost leadership is usually only possible with a lean, efficient organization). It is all the more important that you proceed carefully when determining the corporate strategy.

The corporate strategy and the alignment of the corporate strategy also form the basis for the next chapter in the business plan, marketing.

CHAPTER 19

LAW AND TAXATION

The next step in the business plan is to deal with "Law and Taxes" which is devoted to the topic of which permits are necessary for the establishment, the question of which legal form you can choose for your company, and which company or company name is possible.

The various taxes that arise in self-employment are closely related to the legal form of a company.

Permits, legal form, company name, and taxes

Preparing for the start of a company and setting up a business also includes numerous formalities that need to be processed and clarified, as well as the market analysis or the financial plan. We have prepared these topics for you in the following chapter Law and Taxes. You can then work through these step by step for your business plan.

What permits do you need for your job?

The keywords here are, for example, a license requirement under the trade regulations.

- Which legal form do you choose? In addition to sole proprietorships, partnerships or corporations are available as legal forms of companies.
- Which company name or company name is possible?
- The naming of your company is also linked to the legal form.

- What taxes do you have to pay when you are self-employed?

From income tax to trade tax to sales tax - here too, some taxes in self-employment depend on the legal form chosen.

Obtain permits before starting a business

For most commercial activities you do not need a permit or permit due to the existing freedom of trade. For several activities - especially in the handicrafts or freelancers - a permit is still required or proof of professional qualification must be provided. Special offices, authorities, and institutions should be consulted.

When creating the business plan, you should find out whether you meet the formal requirements for your start-up project. In the Permits section, the activities that require a permit according to the trade regulations.

Which legal form should you choose for self-employment?

The different legal forms of companies result in different requirements for:

The formation process: in particular for formal obligations such as an entry in the commercial register or whether a notary has to be consulted as well as for the time after the establishment (follow-up obligations) such as accounting or the taxes to be paid in self-employment.

You have to decide which legal form suits your company best. In particular, this means weighing up the financial, tax, and legal effects on your future business activities. A distinction is made between the legal forms of companies

- one-man business
- Partnerships
- Corporations

Which company name is possible?

For many founders, at the beginning of their self-employment, the question arises under which name they are allowed to appear outside. There are some rules about the company name and the title of your company. And so, depending on the entry in the commercial register, a distinction is made between the business name and the company name in the company name. As a result, not all founders and companies are allowed to use a real company name.

Your company logo will also depend upon the company name and brand image.

An overview of taxes for the self-employed

As a founder, you should also approach the subject of taxes with the necessary sense of proportion. Taxes represent an economic burden in self-employment and must also be taken into account in financial planning. Taxes in self-employment include income tax, trade tax, corporation tax, or input and sales tax.

It is advisable to seek the services of a professional to get in-depth knowledge about the taxes applicable to your company and business.

CHAPTER 20

OPERATIONAL ORGANIZATION

After you have clarified the legal form for your establishment, this covers further topics of the company organization. This includes information on existing property rights, the location, the founding team, or the value chain. You should also deal with personnel planning and company structure in the section on an operational organization.

However, the scope of the individual sections in the Business Organization depends on their respective importance for your company.

Business organization as a success factor for companies

Numerous definitions can be found in business administration under the keyword organization or business organization. There are numerous approaches to organizing businesses. For start-ups, not all issues of company organization are as important as they are for the company organization of large companies.

In short, the operational organization comprises the processes and structures of your company. However, it is obvious that good organization and coordination of processes also contribute significantly to the success of the start-up for small companies and that some time should be invested in all aspects of business organization.

So that you do not get lost in the theory of company organization, we have listed the most important points in the Business Organization that you should deal with in the business plan. How detailed you are about the operational organization at this point depends on your company and the importance of the respective topic for your business activities and the operational organization. Some topics from the field of company organization may also be omitted for you.

First, get an overview of the relevant topics of the company organization and then work out the central points for your start-up project. At the end of the on operational organization, set up a milestone plan for your business plan.

Mandatory components in the operational organization

The aspect of property rights is not expected directly by many in the company organization. But if property rights such as patents, trademarks, or designs are of particular importance to your company, you should concentrate on them. Investors, in particular, attach great importance to the start-up's core technologies being protected from imitation as far as possible. In this way, in the Business Organization, you specify in particular what exactly should be protected and what the status of the entry is.

Locations in the company organization

An important point in the company organization is the question of location. Particularly in the case of restaurants, shops, research, or servicesion facilities, explanations are required for the operational organization of your business start-up.

Management and founding team

Management or founding team plays a key role in the organization of young companies. For investors and financiers, the people involved are particularly decisive. Prepare information about the management or founding team in the company organization - of course, even if you start alone. Especially when starting a team, you should show who is taking on which tasks for the operational organization.

Personnel Planning

After you have put the focus on the management or the founding team, do not forget information about other personnel concerning the company organization if you are planning to hire employees for your establishment. Personnel planning is therefore an important factor for an operational organization.

Company structure and organization

In the organization of companies, one often finds extensive organizational charts for the operational organization. Certainly, this is often less extensive when it comes to founding the company - but it is impossible to imagine the company organization without it. Present the planned corporate structure and organization in a comprehensible and transparent manner.

Business performance in the business organization

After you have described the formal organizational structure in the Corporate Structure section, the process organization now follows Purchasing necessary equipment and sellig your services. This section of the business organization is also referred to as business performance.

Value chain: beyond the operational organization

The operational organization of the provision of services in your company is often only a small piece of the puzzle in the entire value chain. Place your company in the value chain of the industry.

You will also come across questions of the operational organization later in practice after the establishment. If you are already considering larger capital purchases, consider this in your financial planning now. Overall, business equipment illuminates numerous practical points of business organization.

Milestones to the start

After you have described the essential points of the operational organization in the business plan, finally create a schedule with the milestones up to the start of business activity.

The milestones include the essential things that have to be done on your part and often also relate in particular to operational organization factors. The schedule enables you and the readers of the business plan to assess critical points of the start-up project in the coming months. The question to be answered is whether the operational organization is up to the intended start.

After the business organization to the financial plan

Now that you have created most of the s of your business plan and also given information about the operational organization of your company, you will devote yourself to finances next. In the financial plan, you have to convert your statements on strategy, marketing, and also the business organization into numbers.

CHAPTER 21

FINANCIAL PLANNING FOR THE BUSINESS

From the calculation of sales and costs to liquidity planning and profitability calculation: Founders and entrepreneurs are often faced with the challenge of creating a financial plan for banks or investors. We'll show you how to set up the financial plan and give you tips for creating it. Do you want to work out a financial plan yourself quickly, easily, and without errors? Follow our instructions below:

1. Definition: What is a financial plan?

The financial plan is the heart of every business plan. It presents the company's development in figures and thus provides information as to whether your start-up is also economically viable. At the same time, it shows how much capital is necessary to finance your self-employment or your company.

2. What do I need a financial plan for when starting up?

The business and financial plan is fundamentally important for the decision of banks or investors if you need money for your start-up. Banks often only use the numbers to estimate whether you will be able to repay the loan including interest. A good financial plan is therefore a success factor for the financing of your project. But for you too, the financial plan is an important controlling instrument to keep an eye on the success of the company and to recognize financial risks early, and act. You should therefore invest sufficient time in creating it. The financial plan shows whether your company is developing profitably.

3. Structure: What belongs in the financial plan?

There is no one size fits all template for the financial plan. If you search for templates, examples, or templates for the financial plan on the Internet, you will find a wide variety of structures. We recommend the following structure for the financial plan, which we developed together with banks and investors in our financial plan tool. There the financial plan is structured as follows:

- Sales planning
- Sales-dependent costs (variable costs)
- Operating and running costs including wages and marketing costs
- Establishment costs
- Investments
- Liquidity & capital requirements
- Financing plan
- Profitability calculation

1 Do the sales planning

First, calculate the sales that you will generate with your servicess or services. Here you use the price calculation made in the business plan and estimate how much you will sell in the first weeks, months, and years. Take into account that your offer is new to the market. In practice, the sales figures of newly founded companies initially increase slowly.

2 Capture the cost

Based on the sales development, you can now calculate what costs you expect in the financial planning. The costs that arise in the course of setting up a business include:

The variable or sales-dependent costs: The variable costs include all costs in the company that arises directly in the servicesion or the preparation of your offer. Examples of this are material costs or the purchase of goods.

The fixed costs or operating costs: The operating costs category includes wages and salaries, rent, marketing costs, insurance fees, etc.

The contribution margin calculation is closely related to the cost calculation. The contribution margin of a services shows you what part of the sales revenue remains after deducting the variable costs to cover the fixed costs. Make sure that the contribution margins of the individual servicess are always positive. Then, with increasing sales, all fixed costs will gradually be covered and you will reach the breakeven point - the break-even point.

The comparison of sales and costs automatically results in the income statement (P&L for short) in your financial plan. It reflects the operational development of the operational in your company. At this point, interest and taxes are also taken into account to determine the result.

3 What are the start-up costs?

The start-up costs are incurred before you can start generating sales with your company. These include consulting costs, fees for trademark registration or entry into the commercial register, costs for finding personnel, and expenses for office equipment. The start-up costs can range from a few hundred to several thousand USD and thus have a strong influence on the capital requirements of a start-up. Therefore, check-in detail what start-up costs will be incurred.

4 Plan investments

In addition to the start-up costs, the investments usually represent an extensive item in the financial plan. The amount varies greatly from business model to business model.

Do not only consider the investments that are necessary to get started in the financial plan. In the investment plan, also record the expansion or replacement investments that arise in connection with the business development in the following years. Based on the investments, depreciation is also determined in the income statement.

5 liquidity planning

Now you have almost all the information you need for your liquidity planning. On the one hand, the results of the operative business, as well as the expenses for the foundation and investments, flow into the liquidity planning. On the other hand, you enter your existing start-up capital. On this basis, you can very practically track the development of your account balance in the financial plan. For most start-ups, this is initially in the red. The liquidity planning shows you how high your capital requirement is, which you have to cover externally.

6 Determine capital requirements and draw up a financing plan

Let us assume the following example to determine the capital requirement: You will break even after 13 months. Until then, you have to pre-finance 65,000 USD. The start-up costs and investments at the start amount to 45,000 USD. You bring your start-up capital of 35,000 USD. Then your liquidity planning results in a capital requirement of 75,000 USD. In the financial plan, you must now explain how you will finance it. How much equity do you bring into the company and how much outside capital do you plan for your start-up? You record this in the financing plan.

When you have decided on the respective financing - i.e. equity vs. external capital - you also enter this in the liquidity planning as an inflow so that your account balance is no longer in the negative range and your capital requirement drops to 0 USD. You must always ensure the liquidity of your company.

7 Profitability Calculation

The conclusion of your financial plan is the profitability calculation, which shows the most important key figures of the operative business on an annual basis. The profitability calculation should enable the reader to quickly see at a glance how profitable the start-up is. For this purpose, the profit and loss account is supplemented by various economic parameters, such as contribution margin or gross profit, gross margins.

4. Financial plan template: create the financial plan with a tool

There are numerous Excel templates for the financial plan circulating on the Internet. For users, however, it is often unclear how old the Excel tools are, whether they contain all the important elements and whether all formulas and references work correctly. Errors often only become visible during the preparation of the financial plan, so that a lot of time is lost in processing. The alternative is to set up an Excel financial plan yourself.

5. Tips for a successful financial plan

To create a professional financial plan, consider the following tips:

Realistic planning: It will not help you if you show an ideal scenario for your business start-up with the lowest possible capital requirement in the financial plan. Practice often shows that sales growth is slower and costs in the company are higher. Then you quickly run into liquidity problems.

Consider buffers: A simple tool for realistic planning is to consider a buffer. This shows banks and investors that even more difficult times can be survived.

Ensure traceability and plausibility: A good financial plan is not just about numbers. Explain your forecasts and values so that the numbers are understandable and plausible. Refer to research results and use sources for the financial plan.

No mistakes in the calculations: If possible financiers detect calculation errors in your financial plan, it should be closely related to a positive decision for financing.

Professional impression: Make sure you have an attractive layout and a clear presentation of your financial plan, especially when it comes to the extensive tables. The finance plan PDF is of course very important here.

Don't forget anything: Have you considered all the points from the above structure in your financial plan?

And very important: know your financial plan inside and out. In a bank meeting or with investors, you will be asked for numerous details about your numbers. Here you shouldn't get caught up in leafing through and reading but have answers quickly and precisely at hand.

6. Frequently asked questions about the financial plan

- Why is the financial plan so important?
- What should be in a financial plan?
- Is there a difference between the income statement and liquidity planning?
- How many years does a financial plan have to cover?
- Isn't planning over several years unrealistic?
- Which tool do I use to create a financial plan?
- Is there any subsidized advice for drawing up financial plans?

7. Advice on drawing up a financial plan

Founder coaches and management consultants offer professional help in drawing up financial plans and finding suitable financing. So that founders can also afford this, there are funding programs that cover a large part of the consulting costs. The financial planning is then often part of the business plan creation that you undertake with the consultant.

8. After the foundation: continuous financial planning and controlling

Even after they have been founded, companies regularly create multi-year financial plans, for example when new business areas are to be developed or larger investment projects are to be implemented. These financial plans do not necessarily have to cover the entire company, but can also cover individual areas.

But regardless of whether you are a small or large company, continuous financial planning should be part of the standard repertoire. Often a 1-year plan is made to plan the next fiscal year. It is also important to continuously compare the actual figures with the target figures so that deviations can be recognized quickly and countermeasures can be taken, if necessary, to prevent liquidity bottlenecks.

Bottom line: use tools in your budget to avoid mistakes

As the heart of every business plan, the financial plan represents the measures for corporate development described in advance in figures. Its components provide answers to the following questions:

- When will profits be made? (Profit and loss account)
- How much money will be spent on starting up? (Formation costs)
- What is money invested in? (Investment plan)
- How high is the capital requirement? (Liquidity planning)
- How is the capital requirement financed? (Financing plan)
- How profitable is the company? (Profitability calculation)

A consistent and step-by-step structure that links the individual components with one another is important for a good financial plan.

Many Excel tools are not recommended due to their susceptibility to errors. A financial plan tool can save you a lot of time and helps to create a professional financial plan that you can use to convince banks and investors.

CHAPTER 22

SWOT ANALYSIS

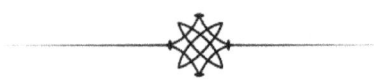

The SWOT analysis is an important part of the business plan. It shows the strengths and weaknesses of a start-up, what the opportunities are and where risks lurk. It is therefore also of interest to banks and investors. The SWOT analysis aims to define measures to be able to use relevant opportunities and minimize major risks.

What is the SWOT analysis?

If you as the founder have worked through chapter by chapter of your business plan, the last important point before the executive summary is the SWOT analysis. On the one hand, it is important to be able to better assess the opportunities and risks of your business model. On the other hand, it is usually demanded and read critically by investors (such as the bank).

SWOT stands for strengths (Strengths), weaknesses (Weaknesses), opportunities (Opportunities), and threats (Threats). The tool, which has been tried and tested for over 50 years, helps founders and companies to identify relevant opportunities and risks with the help of market analysis and competition analysis and to act accordingly.

So that you can make rapid progress with your SWOT analysis, we have put together the most important points for you below.

1. The components of the SWOT analysis

The SWOT analysis is a framework for thinking and analyzing, which should help you as a founder or entrepreneur to stay competitive. It structures the business challenge and helps you, for example, to develop USPs and competitive advantages over the competition.

The SWOT analysis begins with the analysis of the environment and the competitors by asking the following que4stions:

- Which competitors are dangerous?
- What trends, regulations, and laws are there that could be relevant for your company?
- What is the economic and political situation like and does that have an impact on your company?
- This is followed by the strengths and weaknesses analysis of your company

These external influences help you to analyze your strengths and weaknesses. Because a strength or a weakness can never be seen without reference to customer behavior, competition, or other external developments and trends. The key question for you and your SWOT analysis is: "Are we prepared for these external developments?" If you are armed, you have strengths, if you are not, you have weaknesses.

By comparing external trends with strengths and weaknesses, you derive opportunities and risks. An opportunity is given when an external trend meets strength and this allows you to make profitable use of this opportunity.

A risk always arises when an external event threatens your business model and you are unable to counter this threat effectively. For example, the spread of pandemics has become a threat for many businesses, but it is surely a strength for cleaning companies.

Develop measures to make profitable use of opportunities and contain risks

The analysis is good, implementation is better. Once you have discovered opportunities, it is important to use them and implement them profitably. In the case of an identified risk, you need to develop measures to keep the risk small or even turn it into an opportunity. A risk can quickly turn into a corporate crisis.

2. How to easily create your SWOT analysis

You have now got to know the basic principle of SWOT analysis. Now we will show you how to implement your SWOT analysis simply and pragmatically. We recommend a 4-step procedure:

- Step 1: Analyze trends, industry, customers & competitors
- Step 2: Identify strengths and weaknesses
- Step 3: Derive opportunities and risks
- Step 4: develop measures

We will show you the following stages of the SWOT analysis in detail and with corresponding recommendations for action.

Step 1: Analyze trends, industry, customers, and competitors

The first part of the SWOT analysis deals with factors that are and could be relevant to your business model now and in the future - it is about trends.

For your SWOT analysis, write down the most important trends for your industry. It is best to proceed according to the "top-down" variant:

The big trends: First, describe the big trends that may not only be relevant for your market (e.g. demographic change, economic environment, changed consumer behavior, etc.)

Your market: Mention the most important factors that are specifically relevant for your market (e.g. customers are increasingly demanding organic servicess etc.).

Your competitors: Another important factor for the future development of your company is your competitors - what is the competitive situation like (e.g. the top 3 have a market share of 80%, price pressure, etc.)

Your customers: Who exactly are your customers and what do your customers want, what are their needs? Has anything changed in the last few years?

The goal is for you to write down in this part of the analysis all trends that are relevant to your business model and, in particular, maybe in the future. From the abundance of trends, you should filter out 10 to 12 of the most important influencing factors for your company.

With these 10 to 12 trends from the environmental analysis, you can now go into the company analysis.

Step 2 of the SWOT analysis: create a profile of strengths and weaknesses

The analysis of trends from the environment and the industry as well as a well-founded competition analysis are the basis for the analysis of strengths and weaknesses and the derivation of opportunities and risks. The analysis of external trends sensitizes you to derive real strengths and weaknesses in your company from the external trends.

The object of the company analysis as part of the strengths and weaknesses analysis is your company itself. As a rule, you analyze company management, employees, quality of servicess and services, and service quality, as well as things such as location, the efficiency of the organization, and logistics. Financial strength is also the subject of the analysis. Have the most important KPIs from your controlling dashboard ready.

ANALYSIS AREA	KEY QUESTIONS in the SWOT analysis
Corporate governance	Is the team able to successfully face the identified external trends and maneuvers of the competition?
Management experience	Is there enough experience for current and future market trends?
Corporate culture	Are the way of thinking, philosophy and leadership behavior up-to-date with regard to the future trends identified in the market?
Employee	Do we have enough motivated and qualified employees to cope with current and future market trends?
Key roles occupied	What are the key roles against the background of current trends in the market and environment?
qualification	Do you have the necessary qualifications to profitably

	exploit current market trends?
Products and services	Are our products and services attractive in the eyes of customers and are they competitive in comparison to the competition?
Product quality	Do customers praise our products? How is the quality compared to the competition? How are the product reviews?
Service offers	What services does the competition offer? Do our customers praise our service?
Financing offers	How good are our financing offers compared to the competition?
image	Which cult factor do our products have? Are our customers proud to buy our products?
design	Is our design contemporary? Does it suit

	our customers? Do our customers praise it?
Organizational factors	Are the location and quality of the processes and the organization suitable so that we can successfully meet the current trends in the market?
Location	Is our location suitable for working our market effectively and efficiently?
Organizational efficiency	How stable are our processes? Is it stuck somewhere? Are there any problems with service and product quality or employee satisfaction?
logistics	Can we deliver quickly and reliably and inexpensively?
Finances	Are we financially prepared to meet current and future trends?
Financial strength	Can we make the necessary investments ourselves?

Access to capital	Do we get the necessary investments financed at all times?
Profit margin	Is our profit margin so high that we can survive dry spells?
Indebtedness	Does our level of indebtedness influence our ability to act in order to be able to react appropriately to external trends at any time?

How you formulate this catalog of questions as part of your strengths and weaknesses analysis depends on your business model.

Based on these key questions about the strengths and weaknesses analysis in the context of the SWOT analysis, you create your strengths and weaknesses profile.

Advantage: It visualizes the strengths and weaknesses in your company so that you can see at a glance whether you are in a good or bad position.

Step 3: Derive opportunities and risks

After the strengths and weaknesses analysis, take your 10 to 12 most important trends and evaluate them using the strengths and weaknesses profile. This shows whether a trend represents an opportunity or a risk for your company.

Now assign your 5 most important strengths and weaknesses to the three greatest opportunities and risks. If you do this in a table, as shown below, you can already put the first ideas and directions on paper on how to use an opportunity profitably or, conversely, to cushion a risk in the best possible way or even to turn it into an opportunity.

Step 4 of the SWOT analysis: define measures

With the strengths and weaknesses profile, the trends, and the resulting opportunities and risks, you have developed the essential elements of the SWOT analysis.

The next step is to determine the specific actions you can take to reduce the most important risks and take advantage of the opportunities. In this part of the SWOT analysis, write down in detail how you will react to the most important 3-4 risks and which measures you are planning to be able to benefit from the 3-4 opportunities.

You should now budget the planned measures from the SWOT analysis and incorporate them into the financial plan.

3. You should avoid these mistakes in your SWOT analysis

The SWOT analysis is a powerful tool with which you can control your long-term company development. Nevertheless, in practice, there are always typical problems and mistakes that founders or entrepreneurs make in the SWOT analysis.

- the SWOT analysis is too extensive and too complicated
- the analysis leads to an unclear result
- the strengths and weaknesses are not presented honestly
- Opportunities and risks are not recognized
- Strengths and weaknesses are considered independently of customers and competitors

TIP

Your strengths are real when they bring you more customers, directly or indirectly.

CHAPTER 23

THE EXECUTIVE SUMMARY

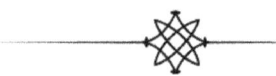

The executive summary, a short and concise summary of the business plan, belongs at the beginning of your business plan. In particular, capital providers, such as banks or investors, often only read the executive summary and then decide whether you want to go deeper into the business plan. The executive summary should only be written after the business plan has been completed.

You should consult an experienced advisor, especially if you want to convince investors with the Executive Summary. The consulting service is usually funded and is therefore worthwhile twice.

Finally, the summary follows

In the executive summary, you present the most important points of your business plan on a maximum of two pages. The executive summary is the summary of your business plan and should arouse interest. The executive summary is particularly important for potential investors and banks, as it enables a good overview of your business model in a short time.

What is an executive summary?

The executive summary is very often referred to as a management summary, as it contains the most important points of a business plan from a management perspective. Accordingly, it is not an introduction to the business plan but rather a summary of your business plan. For this reason, we recommend that you write the executive summary only after the business plan has been completed.

Executive Summary: Your company's business card

The executive summary gives your contact person the first decisive impression. If the executive summary is convincing, the reader usually decides to read through the business plan. Accordingly, the executive summary is very important.

What should be in an executive summary?

On the one, to a maximum of two pages, you have to focus on the essential points of the executive summary. The areas of interest to any investor are the following:

Services (approx. 1/4 page)

Briefly introduce your services/offer and explain who your customers are and where the customer benefits lie.

Market (approx. 1/4 page)

Record why the market is attractive and which important characteristics the industry has.

Goals & Strategy (approx. 1/2 page)

Show which goals you would like to achieve in the short to medium term and which marketing instruments you will use.

Finances (approx. 1/2 page)

The finance plan is of particular interest to investors. Show the financial development of the next 3 years and mention the most important key figures. Do not forget to indicate how high the capital requirements for your business start-up are.

Management (approx. 1/4 page)

The founding team is one of the key factors in the executive summary. A convincing business plan can only be implemented with a strong founding team. In this respect, you should particularly emphasize the specialist, commercial and operational skills, and experience of your founding team.

Who are you writing the executive summary for?

The executive summary allows you to review and highlight the most important points of your business plan - so you write the executive summary for yourself is required and read by potential investors (venture capital companies, business angels, banks, etc.). If the project is judged to be promising based on the executive summary, the business plan is critically examined and then the first meeting usually takes place.

TIP

With the executive summary, you conclude the business plan. Take advantage of the sponsored start-up coaching - an experienced start-up coach will review your business plan and support you with the start-up!

What to look for in the summary

Since the requirements for a highly condensed summary of the business plan are high, you should consider the following points:

Page length: 2 pages maximum.

Since venture capital companies, for example, receive inquiries about financing every day, you should make sure that you keep your summary of the business plan short. On no more than two pages you should try to arouse the interest of the potential investor.

No technical jargon

Write your summary in such a way that a non-specialist person will understand it. Your contacts on the investor side are usually not specialists, so special terms are not helpful. Also, make sure that you avoid lengthy and imprecise wording.

Realistic Assessment

Be realistic about your summary. Sentences like "infinite potential" and "massive increase in profit" seem unprofessional. End the executive summary with a positive outlook.

Position in the business plan

Although the executive summary is written after the business plan has been drawn up, the summary is still at the top of the finished business plan.

The goal is ...... that you formulate a short, concise executive summary that convinces investors and makes them want to read the business plan.

CHAPTER 24

SUM UP ALL TOGETHER.......SET UP YOUR CLEANING COMPANY

With an extensive knowledge on various steps of setting up a business start-up, now let's sum it up by creating your own cleaning company. After studying the basic set-up of a cleaning company, we will also study three types of cleaning businesses in further chapters.

Successful with your own cleaning company

Whether building and facade cleaning, textile cleaning, or even crime scene cleaning - there are many opportunities for specialization as a cleaning company. If you want to open your own cleaning company, it is worth taking a look at the economic development and trends in the industry:

1. Competitive pressure: According to the Federal Guild Association of the Building Cleaning Trade, the building cleaning trade is the busiest in Germany: Every 100th employee works in the building cleaning trade and the trend is increasing. For many of these employed building cleaners, window cleaners, housekeepers, cleaning assistants, and other cleaning staff, starting their own cleaning company with their cleaning crews is a realistic goal. The number of companies active in the cleaning industry is growing accordingly: in 2008 the Federal Statistical Office recorded around 14,000 cleaning companies, in 2015 it was already 21,400. Most of them are small or medium-sized companies.

2. Specialization of small niche providers: According to the Federal Association of Building Cleaners, the range of operations extends from small specialist providers who fill niches in the cleaning and service market to large service companies that offer all services in and on buildings and employ up to 40,000 people in individual cases. With a good 80 percent, most cleaning companies are founded as small businesses and generate only around 15 percent of the industry's turnover with less than 500,000 USD in annual sales. If you want to set up a cleaning company and survive against the competition, you should find a niche and specialize, for example, like a glass cleaner, facade cleaner, maintenance cleaner, hospital cleaner, vehicle cleaner, crime scene cleaner, or construction and building cleaning agent.

The way to self-employment with your own cleaning company

If you want to start your own cleaning company, you need to know how to professionally remove dirt and rubbish without damaging the customer's rooms, objects, and property. He must be familiar with cleaning agents, care servicess, and other chemicals and be able to use appropriate cleaning machines. Besides, building cleaners must observe environmental, waste, and occupational safety laws and be able to assess the dangers to which they, their employees, and customers are exposed in their daily work. In addition to regulations on occupational and operational safety, the ordinance on hazardous substances and, if applicable, the ordinance on organic substances must be observed. And depending on where you clean, strict hygiene regulations apply, for example in hospitals or large kitchens.

But laws and regulations are only one aspect that must be observed on the way to self-employment - careful planning is the other. We will show you the key success factors that are important when starting a cleaning company.

1. Set up a cleaning company with your concept or franchise?

You don't have a coherent concept yourself with which you can set up your own cleaning company as a building cleaner or cleaner? Then franchises can be an interesting alternative for you. There are already numerous franchise systems for specializing in very different cleaning services: Cleanup for cleaning large kitchens, TIDYservice for building cleaning and management, Steinfresh for stone care, or FiltaFry for cleaning deep fryers, for example.

The advantages: As a franchisee, you rely on a tried and tested business model that is already established on the market. You pay a license fee and can rely on the strategy, know-how, and marketing concepts of the franchisor. You benefit from the brand awareness of the franchise concept and territorial protection, among other things. So you can quickly open your cleaning company.

2. Are you an entrepreneur? Recognize your strengths and weaknesses!

Before you start planning and found your cleaning company, analyze your strengths and weaknesses: Find out where your potentials and where risks lie! In this way, you can set specific priorities right from the start and keep an eye on critical factors. With our free start-up test, you can find out how good your prerequisites are for a successful start-up. With the help of 30 questions, the founder test analyzes your strengths and weaknesses and shows you opportunities and risks in detail. The following aspects of the founder test should be dealt with intensively before setting up your own cleaning company:

Personality: Helpful pluses for starting a business and running a company are typical entrepreneurial characteristics such as commitment, willingness to perform, a certain risk tolerance, resilience, self-confidence, leadership qualities, the ability to self-motivate, and the confident handling of stress and setbacks. If you want to start a cleaning company, you should also be very responsible towards your customers and employees.

Motivation: Make yourself aware of why you want to start a business and start a cleaning company:

- Has self-employment been your dream for a long time or has it been a spontaneous idea?
- Are you hoping to earn a higher income as a self-employed building cleaner?
- Are you just looking for a career change or is starting a business a way out of unemployment?

Also, think about the downsides of self-employment:

- Are you ready (at least initially) to invest an above-average amount of time and work in your cleaning company?
- Are you healthy and fit enough to survive long working days (accounting and organization in your own office plus late or even night shifts with customers)?
- Do you have enough capital to set up your cleaning company and purchase the necessary equipment?
- Do you have enough reserves to survive periods of low income?
- Does your partner and/or your family support your step into independence?

Qualification: If you would like to open your own cleaning company, then you should have the appropriate professional experience and qualifications. Training as a building cleaner is not necessary, but it does convey the necessary knowledge in materials science, chemistry, environmental protection as well as the operation and handling of cleaning machines, scaffolding, and work platforms. Also, building cleaners learn special features of the various sub-areas of their trade - such as basic cleaning, carpet cleaning, maintenance cleaning, vehicle cleaning, disinfection measures, and preventive pest control. If you do not have this knowledge, you should hire qualified, competent employees right from the start or set up your cleaning company together with one or more experienced partners.

We will go into more detail in a moment about the special features that result from hazards and risks in building cleaning. In addition to specialist knowledge, basic commercial and business knowledge is important to run your own cleaning company. Attend founding seminars and read specialist literature!

3. Occupational health and safety: dangers and risks in building cleaning

When you start a cleaning company, you have a lot of responsibility for your employees. Simply by handling cleaning agents and using ladders, electrical devices, or scaffolding, you and the employees of your cleaning company are exposed to numerous hazards every day. Hazards in the building cleaning trade arise, for example, from trips to the property to be cleaned, skin contact with cleaning agents, inhalation of vapors from chemicals, noise, e.g. B. by the operation of vacuum cleaners and other electrical devices, as well as the use of these devices and work where there is a risk of falling, in facade cleaning.

As an employer in the building cleaning trade, you must evaluate and document these hazards in an objective risk assessment. You must also, among other things

- Store hazardous substances safely and dispose of them properly,
- Provide your employees with the necessary personal protective equipment (including protective gloves, skin protection agents, and, if necessary, protective goggles),
- Check, maintain and, if necessary, replace work equipment regularly,
- draw up a skin protection plan and

- Observe employment restrictions for young people as well as pregnant and breastfeeding women when handling certain hazardous substances.
- If you want to employ 20 employees or more, you must set up an occupational safety committee following Section 11 of the OSA (Occupational Safety Act), appoint a safety officer, and train company first aiders and fire protection assistants.

TIP

If you want to start a cleaning company, there are numerous dangers for your employees and you. Therefore, check with which insurance you can at least reduce financial risks.

Insurance coverage for your cleaning company

4. Develop a successful business model for your cleaning company!

By now, you already know several things to consider when starting a cleaning company. The next thing you need is a coherent concept. When developing the business model, consider the following nine points:

1 founder

Make yourself aware that you want to start a small business with a cleaning company: What qualifications and experience do you have? Do you have training as a building cleaner? What are your strengths and weaknesses?

2 business idea

What exactly do you want to clean in the future? Private households, offices, clinics, practices, crime scenes, construction sites, vehicles, ships, textiles, carpets, floors, windows, stairs, facades, pipes, or special industrial systems? There is hardly anything that does not have to be cleaned thoroughly now and then - or regularly. Specialization can be a valuable niche for your new cleaning company that bundles competencies, differentiates your company from the competition, and conveys professionalism to customers through specialization.

3 target groups

Who are the customers of your future cleaning company? Usually, the target group already results from your business idea and your specialization. Do not only differentiate between private and commercial customers but go into detail: Analyze important demographic characteristics such as age, place of residence, income, occupation, etc. of your potential customers! What do you need and what customer benefits can your cleaning company offer you?

4 Market & competition

How big are the local market and competition? Is there enough potential for another cleaning company? With Google Maps and Google Search, you will certainly get good results for the first market and competition analysis in your preferred area. But also analyze the concept of the competitors!

5 price & strategy

The subject of the price calculation is a horror for most start-ups. In the building cleaning trade, cheap prices lead to immense price dumping - the only exceptions here are highly specialized areas. To keep up with the prices of the competition and still be able to work profitably, you have to calculate very carefully. Before founding your cleaning company, first, analyze the expenses to be expected: start-up costs, acquisition costs (including for machines, scaffolding, and devices such as high-pressure cleaners, industrial vacuum cleaners, polishing machines), and running costs (including electricity, rent, and salaries). Include the prices of your competitors and industry figures in your pricing.

6 Marketing & Sales

When developing your business model, think about how you want to do marketing to make your cleaning company known and new customers become regular customers. Don't underestimate the potential of recommendations and word of mouth - on the internet and in "real life"!

7 revenue

List the individual services of your cleaning company such as B. window cleaning in private apartments and houses, office, glass, and stairwell cleaning in commercial properties such as offices or practices and estimate the number of your potential customers, for example, based on industry key figures, their cleaning intervals and the time you see the customers Place each will be realistic. This gives you further essential components for your price calculation.

8 Ongoing Operating Costs - Operating Costs

When designing the concept, consider the running costs a cleaning company incurs. The most important types of costs are:

Cost of goods: purchase of cleaning agents and smaller devices

Personnel costs: wages and salaries for your employees and your entrepreneur's wages

These costs must be covered by the prices of your cleaning services.

9 resources

Important resources of your cleaning company are your machines and devices, in some of which a lot of capital is tied up, and above all your employees. Think carefully about whether you want to rely on unskilled laborers to keep up with the price dumping in the cleaning industry, or whether at least in some areas qualified specialists will pay off.

5. Business and financial plan: The detailed planning for your cleaning company

Is your business model in the towel? Then you can now work out all the details of your cleaning company in a detailed business and financial plan and subject them to an initial critical review. You not only need a business plan and financial plan to keep track of your income and expenses as well as important key data such as the location, staff, and advertising of your cleaning company. They are also the central planning tools that banks and other financiers want to see to examine your project. Planning is easy with our free business plan software. This guides you step by step through all chapters and supports you with key questions about the content: Use business plan software now!

But what exactly does the business plan have to contain? Here we go into the central content. You can take much of this from your previously developed business model and specify it:

1 legal form

Have you already thought about whether you want to set up your cleaning company as a sole trader or with partners? When choosing the legal form, tax and liability aspects, as well as your start-up capital, are decisive. With us, you will find more information on the legal forms of a sole proprietorship, GbR, UG / Mini-GmbH, and GmbH as well as other partnerships and corporations with which you can set up your cleaning company.

2 location for your cleaning company

With your cleaning company, you do not have to rely on walk-in customers, because you perform your services at the customer's site. That means you do not need a central location for your office and the storage rooms of your machines. A cheap commercial area on the outskirts of the city can therefore be a good choice, as every penny counts under competitive pressure. When choosing the location, however, make sure that you can easily reach your customers from there. To ensure short distances and travel times, you should not sit too far away from your customers.

3 recruiting: attracting employees to your cleaning company!

Unskilled temporary workers can certainly also take on some of the tasks in your newly opened cleaning company. But do not underestimate the support that trained specialists can offer you, especially in the early days after the company was founded. This is particularly true in areas in which you still lack the necessary know-how and routine - perhaps in accounting or when using special cleaning processes

4 Financial Plan: Determine the capital needs for your cleaning company

How much capital you need to start your business depends not least on the type of cleaning company you want to open. If you limit yourself to cleaning the interiors of private households, offices, or medical practices, for example, you probably do not need such expensive equipment as if you were to e.g. B. specializes in the cleaning of construction sites or industrial plants. There is therefore no general answer as to how much it will ultimately cost you to set up your cleaning company. However, the following overview shows you for which items you have to plan one-off start-up costs and start-up costs, and for which you will later incur regular costs when your cleaning company operates:

Cost type	Details
Foundation costs / startup costs	Business plan and financing advice

	Logo, website, and corporate design
	Trademark registration
	Business registration, possibly articles of association, an entry in the commercial register, notary fees
	Possibly broker and compensation payments
	Advertising measures for the opening (advertisements, flyers)
Investments	
	Furniture (including office: desk, computer, printer), devices (including vacuum cleaners, high-pressure cleaners, polishing machines) as well as equipment (including ladders, scaffolding, lifting platforms, containers, buckets, brooms) and work clothing (including protective equipment,

	gloves, safety glasses, hearing protection)
	Original equipment consumables
	Later repair and replacement of facility, appliances, equipment, and protective gear
Running costs	Rent of office space and storage space
	Insurance (including public liability, occupational disability, and health insurance)
	Labor costs and social security contributions for your cleaning staff as well as your company wages
	Electricity, water, heating, telephone, and internet
	Contributions (including IHK, trade association)
	Consumables (e.g. cleaning agents, care servicces, chemicals, lubricants,

	cleaning rags, sponges, polishing floss)
	Advertising and marketing
	Advice (e.g. tax advisor)

5 secure funding

Using your financial plan, you can see how much equity you have to start your cleaning company and how much debt you need to borrow. For the latter, it is now important to find suitable financing options. With your business and financial plan, you can search for lenders in a targeted manner. Also, check financing options through government grants and funding programs as well as cheap funding from KfW.

6 Publicity: Promote Your Cleaning Company!

Rely on a professional website right from the start, place advertisements in the local print media, and distribute flyers to your target group! And so that your cleaning company is easily found online when searching for cleaning companies in your city, you should also add the location of your Google My Business page care for. The Google location entry is not only useful for local searches, but it also allows customers to rate and recommend your cleaning company and your offer. Also think of entries in the yellow pages, online business directories, and service portals such as myhammer.de and helpling.de. And don't underestimate the effect of discount campaigns, loyalty points, and special offers. In this way, you can draw attention to your offer even before you open your cleaning company.

6. Starting your cleaning company - practical and formal

Have your cleaning company's business concept and business plan in place? Great, you have already completed the essential tasks for your business start-up. But before you can open your cleaning company, some administrative procedures and formalities such as registering a business and opening a business account have to be completed. Also think about taking out important insurance: Because you and your employees work in your customers' offices. Something can happen quickly and your customers' property can be damaged while cleaning. Or someone slips on the freshly cleaned floor and breaks a leg. Without appropriate insurance, you bear the financial risk - and thus unnecessarily put your young company out of play.

We have summarized everything in a clear checklist for you so that you do not forget any important founding steps and administrative procedures.

CHAPTER 25

BECOME A SELF-EMPLOYED CLEANING CONTRACTOR

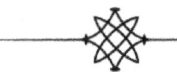

Creating a cleaning business as a self-employed person is an excellent solution to launch your activity while enjoying the advantages of self-employed status. However, it is necessary to take certain steps before launching your self-employed cleaning business.

Creating a cleaning company: is the status of auto-entrepreneur possible?

To create a cleaning business, it is quite possible to choose the status of auto-entrepreneur. This is easy to obtain and offers great flexibility to the worker. The auto-entrepreneur in cleaning can thus start to develop his activity and grow his business.

Becoming a self-employed person in the field of cleaning can be interesting for the employer insofar as the latter does not pay employer contributions and can benefit from certain tax breaks in certain cases. Thus, the status of auto-entrepreneur is not only possible but also recommended to meet a specific demand.

However, if starting a cleaning business with the status of a self-employed person is quite possible, there are some things to keep in mind. First, the establishment of a clientele is entirely due to the auto-entrepreneur. In other words, the auto-entrepreneur will have to invest in sales canvassing and prospecting to find customers.

Note: the prospecting time is a time for which it is impossible to obtain income. However, we are seeing the emergence of new networking companies in the field of personal services, more particularly concerning cleaning.

On the other hand, the person wishing to set up a cleaning business should also be aware that companies may take time to settle certain services (generally around a month). Before getting started, it is, therefore, necessary to have a small amount of capital to make the first purchases and to have sufficient funds for daily life during the first days of the activity.

The steps to take to clean as a self-employed person

To be able to clean as a self-employed person, you have to carry out the same steps as all self-employed persons. Thus, it is first necessary to complete the self-employed person declaration using the dedicated P0 AE form available free online. You must attach to the latter a photocopy or a scan of proof of identity bearing the following mention: "I certify on my honor the accuracy of this proof of identity", followed by the place and date of Signature.

You should also know that you can use the help of a professional such as LegalPlace to help you in your creative process. You just need to fill out an online form, we take care of everything from your online entry to your business creation.

Once these elements have been gathered and sent, the administration will communicate to the auto-entrepreneur all the elements necessary for the exercise of his activity. Thus, the self-employed person in the cleaning industry as well as the self-employed cleaning lady will receive their SIRET number and notification of their tax regime. This information will be accompanied by the contact details of the fiscal contacts of the tax center on which the self-employed person in cleaning depends.

Pros and cons of starting a cleaning business as a self-employed person

Advantages: flexibility and flexibility

One of the advantages of the status of auto-entrepreneur for a person carrying out a cleaning activity is the compatibility of the status with a salaried activity. In other words, the person will be able to have additional income by combining his salary with his activity. This is an important element in the event of a reduced schedule.

Also, cleaning takes time, and this is precious for the self-employed in cleaning who, in addition to having to canvass and retain customers, will have to perform their cleaning tasks. The auto-entrepreneur status has the advantage of being relatively flexible and freeing the auto-entrepreneur from certain administrative obligations. No need to keep detailed accounts or to accomplish many formalities, the status of auto-entrepreneur is very flexible and thus allows the person carrying out a cleaning activity to dedicate himself only to his work.

The main advantage of the status of auto-entrepreneur for a person carrying out a cleaning activity is the possibility of working both for companies and for individuals. Thus, by combining these two clienteles, the auto-entrepreneur can develop two parallel sources of income. If such an operation may appear delicate, it allows the self-employed to develop his activity and his clientele. This can be a very effective process, especially at the start of your business.

Finally, the last advantage of the auto-entrepreneur status for a person carrying out maintenance activities lies in the flexibility of the status. The self-employed person can choose their clients and schedules and thus adapt their workload according to their needs while working for a variety of companies, organizations, and people.

Disadvantages: VAT and the capital exemption

One of the major drawbacks is that the auto-entrepreneur is exempt from VAT. In other words, he does not charge VAT to his customers but also cannot recover it on his purchases, which can be detrimental to him. Indeed, it must be taken into account that purchases, in the field of cleaning, occupy a particularly important place in the expenses of the contractor (purchase of numerous consumables (sponges, mops, cleaning servicess, etc.) and accessories (brooms vacuum cleaners, squeegees, etc.)). To this must be added the travel expenses. Taken together, all of these purchases may ultimately represent particularly significant costs for the entrepreneur and from which he will not be able to recover anything.

On the other hand, for people working under the status of auto-entrepreneur in a cleaning activity, it is important to remember that they are subject to a turnover limit. In the case of a self-employed person in cleaning, this ceiling is $ 33,200 per year. Ultimately, this is a ceiling that can be reached quickly after a few months of operation, when the entrepreneur's customer base is developed.

Another disadvantage, and not the least: in the context of retirement contributions, the quarters validated are only based on a specific turnover. Thus, in 2018, you must have achieved a turnover of at least 2320 $ per year to validate a quarter. This element may appear marginal but it may prove to be important for a person wishing to supplement his income with self-employed activities and who does not have sufficient time to accumulate such a sum of money.

Finally, declaring yourself a self-employed person can be a barrier when it comes to obtaining financing from financial institutions. The majority of banks are generally reluctant to grant loans or financial largesse to solely self-employed people. To cope with this difficulty, it is possible to keep your tax returns to prove a certain standard of living and, possibly, a certain heritage.

It is important to take into account all of these disadvantages before embarking on this activity. Indeed, each of them corresponds to a difficulty that the entrepreneur will encounter as his cleaning business develops. That being said, the many advantages of being a self-employed person in cleaning are also important and reduce the impact of these disadvantages.

CHAPTER 26

SELF-EMPLOYED AS A GENERAL CLEANER

Anyone who wants to become self-employed as a cleaner should attach great importance to a literal, 'clean' strategic business orientation right from the start. Overall, the industry is fiercely competitive, which of course brings with it a certain price pressure. In contrast, there is a large potential target group with numerous companies and many private households for permanent orders. For orientation: In 2015, according to the Federal Statistical Office, sales in this sector were just under 16 billion dollars. In the following article, all essential factors for a successful path to self-employment as a cleaning agent are to be highlighted. In general, self-employment in this area allows for a higher income, as the salary in salaried employment is rarely not far from the statutory minimum wage. This area is about the professional cleaning of sanitary facilities and floors. Cleaners are often used by companies, especially in offices. In the private sector, cleaning activities can extend to all living spaces.

To start with, prospects should ask themselves whether they want to start an entire home care business or try their hand at a one-man business. The latter has the advantage that less capital is required and the overall risks are also lower. However, the range of services of a one-man company can quickly reach its limits. Of course, a location analysis must also be included in the decision: What is the competitive situation on-site? How big is the potential clientele in the private and commercial sector? Up to which radius does an action radius still, make economic sense? If a company is to be founded, business premises and a vehicle fleet should also be considered. In the case of the one-man company, the available space may be sufficient to stow work utensils.

Job-specific requirements in the compact summary

Since the profession of cleaning is not protected, no vocational training is a prerequisite for becoming self-employed. It should not be left unmentioned, however, that sound professional experience and industry knowledge are certainly a great advantage for the step into self-employment, especially when it comes to calculating offers and estimating time. After all, the services provided must be based on market standards, but still enable a satisfactory level of income. And qualitative aspects also appear to be very important to build up a customer base or to retain regular customers over the long term. This creates a more or less reliable income base after a difficult start-up phase.

Determine the basic business direction and consider the consequences

The opportunity to the private or commercial sector specializes, the site will certainly be a decision-making tool. The analysis should be based on numbers or facts, if possible, to determine how great the demand is for a particular room care service. The solvency of the targeted target group certainly also plays a role. In general, the field of activity of the cleaner is broad, so that specializations can also be useful to stand out in the customer perception with a strong added value. One could think of professional carpet cleaning, for example. It should be noted that the strategic business orientation also has consequences for working hours: In the commercial sector, for example, the working hours are mainly in the evenings or on weekends. While commercial spaces are usually cleaned daily, weekly use can be sufficient in private households. This means that for the specialization in the commercial sector there seems to be no alternative to founding a company due to the resources alone, especially since larger companies only rarely cooperate with lone fighters in this area.

Calculation of the financial security

Since the start-up phase is usually financially difficult, it is important to establish a reliable basis with a well-thought-out business plan. Besides, a business plan is always a professional calling card for your business idea. If you want to convince external donors, you should therefore leave nothing to chance when working out it. It is also important to consistently examine all possible financial support options to keep the entrepreneurial leeway as large as possible. When calculating prices or customer-specific offers, not only the essential factor "working time" has to be calculated. Ancillary costs to be covered must also be included along with the targeted profit margin. In this sense, professional liability insurance is of great importance, because cleaning can always lead to accidental damage. The operating materials such as cleaning materials and work utensils must also be taken into account. A used or leased vehicle also generates costs; in the case of a company, a small fleet can quickly come together here. Anyone who rents business premises must also have fixed monthly costs on their bill. Of course, you should always think about private insurance, with health and pension insurance being given top priority.

Formal requirements for a 'clean' business start-up

Regardless of whether it is a one-man housekeeping service or starting a business, the state sets a formal framework that will take up additional time and financial resources. There should be clarity about this from the start so that there is no quick disenchantment in everyday working life. In addition to the job, accounting also takes on a daily role by writing invoices and posting payments. Anyone who does not have in-depth commercial knowledge should involve a tax advisor to act as advantageously as possible and, above all, in compliance with the law. This creates additional costs, but your resources can be used consistently for the essentials. And that is the committed management of one's economic existence. To be able to start business operations, business registration with the locally responsible trade office is required. The background to this is that it is a permanently profit-oriented activity. This also results in the obligation to pay trade tax, but only from an annual tax exemption of currently just under 25,000 dollars. Incidentally, the amount of the trade tax results from the assessment rate, which can vary greatly from city to city. In this respect, this not insignificant factor should also be taken into account in the necessary location analysis.

Put customer acquisition on a sustainable basis right from the start

The company is in the market after all the necessary formalities, but the customers will certainly not come in droves by themselves. In this respect, targeted marketing activities should be high on the company agenda from the start. In the age of the omnipresent Internet, a search engine optimized homepage appears to be indispensable to be available to potential customers around the clock or to offer a professional contact point. Traditional newspaper advertisements can also be an effective approach. Ultimately, it also depends on a strong network to get new customers. This is how we cooperate with other home care companies to consider. However, if you are a self-employed person who accepts orders from other companies/providers, you should avoid possible bogus self-employment be careful, which is not uncommon in this industry. The criterion of being bound by instructions is decisive here. Self-employed cleaners should therefore not be bound by instructions and work in their name and account. In this respect, independent cleaners who enter into cooperation must not be firmly integrated into the work or process organization of clients. Ultimately, convincing work results and satisfied customers will 'automatically' ensure recommendations and a growing customer base. Here we come full circle to the quality mentioned, which appears to be essential for sustainable business success.

Summary with practical relevance: to become a successful self-employed cleaner

The cleaning industry is highly competitive with correspondingly high price pressure. With sales in the two-digit billion range, the business opportunities are turning out to be very promising

Consider basic strategic direction: private vs. commercial area? / One-man operation or company foundation?

Location analysis: how big is the competition? How big and the solvent is the intended target group?

Added value / unique selling point through specialization (e.g. carpet cleaning, etc.). Vocational training is not required, but relevant professional experience and industry knowledge are strongly recommended

When calculating the price, do not just calculate the time factor, but all costs incurred for business operations and personal security. Before starting business operations, a business registration must be made

Put customer acquisition on a broad basis right from the start: Homepage, advertisements, cooperations, etc.

CHAPTER 27

BECOMING SELF-EMPLOYED AS A BUILDING CLEANER

If you don't just literally come to terms with yourself and want to dare to reorient your career, you should consider the option of starting your own business as a building cleaner. In general, there is the option of running your own company with employees or a one-man company as a mobile cleaner with a permanent customer base. Basically, as with any business start-up, the basis for economic success is laid in advance through holistic and conscientious planning. In the following article, important factors in this regard will be examined in a practice-oriented manner.

Basics for introductory orientation

The building cleaner is a state-recognized and therefore legally protected training occupation. If you want to use this official name, you have to be able to show that you have had specialist training or you have to use an alternative name. Specifically, it is a craft occupation in which a master's degree can be aspired to. However, this is not a prerequisite for the step into self-employment. However, it can prove to be an advantage on the free market to stand out from the cheap competition. Right from the start, entrepreneurs should think carefully about the difficult environment: The building cleaning trade is the busiest in The world. In this respect, the competitive situation is very greatly depending on the location.

More importantly, the price war is very tough. Since these are usually not very high-priced services, start-ups have little room for maneuver when it comes to prices. In general, however, self-employed building cleaners can earn significantly more than salaried colleagues. For the latter, the industry-relevant minimum wage applies, which will rise from March 2016, for example for glass and facade cleaning in the western world, to 12.98 dollars (11.10 dollars in the east). Here, entrepreneurs can already get an impression of the wage costs to be expected. However, wages vary depending on the area of work. The self-employed should consider whether the prices are calculated according to the time factor or per unit to be cleaned. The latter option would have direct added value for customers, to be able to calculate the final costs immediately. The entrepreneurial risk (the time factor) would then remain with the building cleaner. In any case, the prices should be based on local standards.

Requirements for self-employment as a building cleaner

There is no obligation to be a master in this craft. If you want to officially call yourself a building cleaner, you need state-recognized training. To be able to start a business activity, a trade must first be registered. Only with the trade license obtained do entrepreneurs have the formal legitimation for self-employment in their hands. As part of the business registration, the activities offered are described as comprehensively and precisely as possible. At this point, entrepreneurs also have to state on paper whether they want to set up a company with employees or a one-man company.

A clear perspective is a basic requirement for every successful building cleaner

It is of strategic importance to get the cleaning company right at the start. Should only private customers be served? Or is the focus on business customers (companies, offices, doctor's offices, etc.)? Of course, the range of services should also be described in detail or adapted accordingly. Depending on the needs in the area and your abilities, it can either be broadly based or occupy a niche that has not yet been covered in the surrounding area (e.g. professional facade cleaning, cleaning of floor coverings, etc.). The specific strategic direction depends primarily on the local demand, which should be analyzed in as much detail as possible in advance. At the same time, the business radius should be defined: Up to what maximum distance can order be accepted? What about the travel costs? Are jobs X kilometers away even worthwhile?

- Overview: possible services/specializations for independent building cleaners
- Basic orientation: private or commercial?
- holistic building cleaning (complete solutions)
- Facade cleaning
- glass cleaning
- Specialization in industrial cleaning (e.g. cleaning of plants)
- Textile cleaning (carpets)
- professional clinic cleaning
- Construction site cleaning

Your own experience and specialist knowledge as well as a detailed market analysis allow you to choose your strategic direction. You always have to consider how great the demand is in the region, how financially strong (and willing!) Customers are and how the immediate competitive situation is. Since this is a highly competitive market, it is important to position yourself as unique in the customer's perception. This attractive added company value can also be linguistically reflected in the company name for effective services placement.

How extensive should self-employment be?

Anyone who becomes self-employed as a mobile specialist must 'only' take care of themselves. If you want to build up an entire company, you have to do a lot more time-consuming tasks at the beginning: an office and capable and reliable employees have to be found, possibly a vehicle fleet should be considered. The wages have to be earned, which is not always easy in the difficult start-up phase. In this respect, well-thought-out financial planning plays an important role. Ideally, a certain amount of equity can also be brought in. The choice of legal form is a first step to limit possible corporate liability risks. Those who only want to be responsible for themselves and organize their time independently will certainly do better with the 'smaller' solution of setting up a business in this area.

Proactively avoid unnecessary risks for the established cleaning company

Shavings fall wherever planning takes place: it is not uncommon for glass to break or stains caused by aggressive cleaning agents that are not used properly. Damage can occur wherever building cleaners work. These should be covered by a high-performance business liability insurance to protect yourself against excessive additional burdens, especially in the financially sensitive start-up phase. And even in professional communication with customers, it can only be seen as an advantage that any damage is insured.

Conclusion: business success against the background of customer acquisition and a necessary environmental analysis

Even if the market is very large and highly competitive, it continues to grow: More and more companies and private individuals (in The world more and more pensioners live as potential solvent customers!) Use professional cleaning services. If you want to be successful, you have to place yourself skillfully in your environment. This applies to both company founders and lone fighters in terms of services and prices. Thorough work results are the basis for satisfied and thus loyal customers so that a tribe with steady orders can gradually be built up. Excellent work results also made the free, but very effective, word-of-mouth advertising active. The Internet can provide an alternative way of customer acquisition with a search engine optimized website.

Flyers, image brochures, entries in relevant online portals, and advertisements in daily newspapers can be effective marketing tools to attract customers' attention.

What seems to be particularly important ...

All in all, it seems very important to set yourself apart from the competition through thorough professionalism right from the start. A first-class and comprehensive service is also an effective means of being able to enforce higher prices than the cheap competition. Low prices to get to know are a possible way to get new customers. In the long term, however, entrepreneurs deprive themselves of the basis for satisfactory income through a cheap strategy. If the thoroughness has to be saved at some point, the downfall of the company will not belong in coming. However, if you know how to professionally familiarize customers with this craft, the willingness to pay higher prices also increases.

Becoming self-employed as a building cleaner: an overview of key success factors

- the training occupation building cleaner is state-recognized and protected
- Environmental analysis/appreciation of the starting prerequisites: this commercial sector is one of the largest in The world, consequently the competition and, above all, price pressure is enormous
- Business registration is mandatory for self-employed workers in this area (however, there is no requirement for a master craftsman for this trade)
- Define basic strategic direction: private or commercial customers? Set up a one-man business or cleaning company? Which services should be offered (=> unique selling point? Perceived added value from the customer's point of view?)

- Define the perimeter of the business orientation: Up to what maximum distance should a mobile cleaning service be used to catch customers?
- Thorough professionalism: convincing work results are the best calling card for activating the important word-of-mouth propaganda.

CHAPTER 29

SELF-EMPLOYED AS A WINDOW CLEANER

Setting up a business as a window cleaner: In many households there are several windows to clean, but enthusiasm for this cleaning activity is often limited. There is, even more, to do in the commercial and public sectors, because large buildings often have huge glass and window surfaces that need to be cleaned regularly. After all, there is no second chance for a first impression. This is exactly where independent window cleaners come into play, who ideally stand for streak-free shine including a high level of service orientation. But what should be considered to become self-employed as a professional window cleaner? Which strategic considerations and formal requirements have to be considered? What is the prospect of success in this area? These and other questions are to be pursued in the following technical article in a practice-oriented and action-oriented manner.

Introductory overview and demarcation from the professional field of building cleaning

The special field of activity of the window cleaner belongs to the job description of the building cleaner. But while a building cleaner is familiar with all cleaning work in and on buildings, the window cleaner specializes in glass surfaces. So not only windows and glass doors are cleaned, but also glass external facades, as are often found in large office buildings in particular. In this respect, specialization within the cleaning industry is already carried out through this field of activity.

Take environmental conditions into account: the strong competition in the cleaning industry

It should be noted that the building cleaning sector, with a good 600,000 employees, is one of the largest trades in the world. The local competition is correspondingly great and the pressure on prices is enormous. The statutory minimum wage or an agreed minimum wage applies to employed window cleaners. Anyone who works independently as a window cleaner will have to earn higher hourly wages, after all, in addition to working hours and the use of materials, the running costs for living costs and social security must be covered (think of the costs for health insurance and private pension provision).

The costs or final prices for customers should be calculated realistically. In the long run, competitive prices are not a solution to putting the business on a sustainable basis. Customers can be attracted by this, but your profit situation will hardly be able to reach a satisfactory level. It should also be borne in mind that prices also influence the perceived quality. Depending on the intended target group, higher fees can also be charged.

Market analysis and determination of the range of services

Due to the sometimes enormous competitive situation, a meaningful location analysis is essential at the beginning. What needs to be discussed is how many competitors there are concerning the intended target group. This can be used to roughly estimate how large the potential order situation is. As far as the target group is concerned, it has to be decided in principle whether only private or also commercial customers should be targeted.

It is also conceivable to work with public clients. But since they often make public tenders for the award of contracts, the price pressure is enormous. The location- or market analysis can therefore show that the demand for a certain target group is greater. Also, it is important to consider which radius of action should be chosen or which is still economically viable. Does it pay off to accept orders with a journey of more than 50 kilometers? The following questions summarize all essential factors in this area:

1. How big is the intended target group?

2. How big is the demand in the defined action radius?

3. How many companies/competitors are there already (=> Internet research)?

4. What services do competitors offer at what prices?

Answering these basic questions allows you to strategically position your offer concerning the location as intelligently as possible.

Business plan writing: This formal guidance sets the business direction

The business basics need to be worked out long before the first window is cleaned. The described market and location analysis is an essential part of a business plan to be worked out. In this, the planning of the finances plays an important key role. Only those who plan realistically and well-founded with their finances will be able to convince external financiers of the business idea. In the business plan, founders are also 'forced' to answer important questions for business success:

Unique selling point: What makes the company particularly attractive from the customer's point of view or compared to the competition?

Marketing and customer acquisition: how can customers be effectively reached?

Price calculation: Which prices are attractive for customers and business start-ups?

For many aspiring self-employed, such strategic or commercial questions are a major challenge, especially if specific specialist knowledge is not (yet) available. In this case, it is advisable to use a professional template for a business plan. This ensures that all relevant content is processed in the correct form. To eliminate deficits in the area of corporate management, it is advisable to attend start-up seminars or special coaching sessions at an early stage. In these training measures, relevant practical knowledge is conveyed in a short time.

A clean affair? Honestly assess the personal requirements for this profession

Following on from the above thought, it must be clear to independent window cleaners that the actual manual activity makes up the main focus but is expanded to include another facet in everyday working life. We're talking about accounting including receivables management or commercial tasks in general. Invoices must be written and incoming payments checked. The costs must always be kept in view so that the liquidity that is so important for entrepreneurial action is retained.

Also, the person starting prerequisites for self-employment as a window cleaner must be honestly assessed, because the personal and financial risks are greater compared to employment. The job is physically demanding, often working outside or at lofty heights (facade cleaning). The handling of chemical cleaning agents can also pose a certain risk to health in the long term (sound knowledge for proper use is therefore essential).

Besides, a joy in dealing with people is essential, because as a window cleaner you will have to deal with a wide variety of clients every day. Quite a few will take a critical look at the work results. A convincing quality will be important to be able to retain customers permanently. Word-of-mouth propaganda will certainly play an important role, especially in the private customer sector.

Formal requirements for starting a business as a window cleaner

To be self-employed as a window cleaner, a trade must be registered before starting the business activity. In the course of business registration, the range of services offered to customers must be described as precisely and comprehensively as possible. For this manual activity, simple business registration is usually sufficient, as there is no separate requirement for a permit. In general, the trade of building cleaning does not require a license, so that no master's degree is required for business registration as the basis for self-employment. The barriers to entry are therefore very low, so that career changers in this area can also successfully advance their professional independence.

Career prospects: Training and further education opportunities for window cleaners

In addition to specialist training as a building cleaner, several further training measures can be considered, for example, to strategically focus on special building types or cleaning processes (and thus to be able to offer customers a unique selling point). A short internet search is sufficient to get an initial overview in this regard. A university degree in engineering in hygiene and cleaning management can also be an option (also to expand the range of services).

Business risks should be known at an early stage

When working on or with glass, damage cannot be ruled out, as a small amount of inattention is often enough. In this respect, self-employed window cleaner should a business liability insurance arm for such cases. It should be noted that this activity is also subject to seasonal fluctuations, which can have a direct impact on income. In a harsh winter with freezing temperatures, the outside will not be able to be cleaned. In this respect, financial reserves must always be formed for such cases. Due to the physically demanding work, a statutory or private insurance tariff with daily sickness allowance is strongly recommended. To secure one's workforce as the most important asset for self-employment, disability insurance can be an option worth considering.

Conclusion for the path to self-employment as a window cleaner

Due to the low entry barriers (license-free craft without a master craftsman's obligation), lateral entrants can also quickly get started on self-employment as a window cleaner. However, this industry with the largest number of employees in The world is characterized by enormous competition, which results in high price pressure. There should be clarity about this. In this respect, a thorough market and location analysis with a tailored offer design is an essential success factor for sustainable business success.

Becoming self-employed as a window cleaner: Summary with relevant key aspects

Trade must be registered for this self-employed activity (before the actual start of business activity, this also applies to an ancillary trade)

Low entry hurdles: This is a non-licensed craft activity without a master craftsman's obligation

The strategically smart positioning of your specialist services: The tense competitive situation in this high-turnover industry requires a conscientious analysis of the initial situation

With a fully developed business plan, all areas of the business model are worked out in a target-oriented manner. Finances, in particular, should be carefully planned.

CHAPTER 29

BECOME SELF-EMPLOYED AS A GRAFFITI CLEANER

Sometimes start-ups just have to keep their eyes open or walk through the street to find a promising business idea. It is not uncommon in The world that one morning homeowners discover colorful and eye-catching graffiti on a wall or facade. What the sprayer wanted to showcase as an effective work of art causes nothing but anger for the homeowner. The wish that this smear should be removed as quickly as possible and completely without residue shoots up in him. It is precisely at this point that the demand for the business idea presented here, ' self-employed as a graffiti remover', comes into play.

What does graffiti mean?

The word originally comes from Latin. It means something like scratching. It is true that 'artists' spray graffiti these days. In its original form, however, the term refers to ancient cave paintings.

Who removes graffiti?

This is a key question that targets the core of this business idea. Apart from painting companies and cleaning methods, few specialists have specialized entirely in the niche of graffiti removal. The term niche should not be misunderstood: it is expressly not an indication of a small demand, on the contrary. In the analysis of the starting position, figures are to be presented that represent an attractive market with high sales in the three-digit million range. And when you take a walk

206

through streets in major German cities, you quickly see that graffiti is a common problem.

Analysis of the initial situation

In this first chapter, relevant business factors for planning are presented, which are then ultimately to be brought to the point in the business plan in a potential-oriented manner. In general, the image of graffiti in The world is bad from the point of view of those affected. Anyone who does not belong to the sprayer scene will not be able to gain anything from this form of art. This is a clear indication of the sustainable opportunities of the business idea 'become self-employed as a graffiti remover'. Homeowners, companies and regional transport companies, and especially Deutsche Bahn spend millions of dollars every year to remove graffiti. Business founders can earn money from this revenue cake if they successfully set up their graffiti removers.

Why is there graffiti?

Whether it is art or graffiti is certainly entirely up to the beholder. The graffiti scene in New York has its origins in 1968. It was a more or less artistic protest against the establishment. It is a figurative-artistic form of expression. Even today, sprayers primarily want to generate attention and often also share (politically motivated) messages with many people. Of course, graffiti is not a trivial offense, but purely legally damage to property. Sprayer caught will face criminal prosecution. Unless the client explicitly wants to embellish walls or garages with individual graffiti. There are of course such examples. You do not belong to the target group of this business idea (unless the client can no longer stand the image after a few years).

Why have graffiti removed (professionally!)?

Graffiti experts emphasize that the images or sayings should be removed as soon as possible. Not only to protect the substance and prevent long-term damage. The main thing is not to offer sprayers the attention or projection surface that they want. Those affected are advised to have graffiti removed by experienced professionals. Anything else can result in a lot of work and expensive follow-up costs if the substance under the graffiti is damaged by the attempts to remove it. Professional graffiti removers, for example, use special chemical cleaning agents or powerful high-pressure cleaners.

Anyone who wants to earn money removing graffiti can only see unsightly graffiti in it. Figures show that hundreds of millions of dollars are spent every year in The world to professionally remove graffiti. Deutsche Bahn in particular spends many millions of dollars every year to have trains freed of unwanted lettering or images.

What do the statistics say about the assessment of the dimensions?

Is graffiti an attractive target market with the prospect of a good long-term order situation? If you look at the statistics, this question can be answered with a resounding yes. According to statista.com, there have been significantly more than 100,000 recorded cases of property damage through graffiti in The world over the past 10 years. In the last two years, the value has fallen slightly below 100,000, which still speaks for a good order situation as a graffiti remover. The chances for the chosen location or radius of action must be concretized.

Work out a business plan as a graffiti remover

This business idea can be classified in the area of professional or commercial cleaning services. If entrepreneurs do not want to market themselves as cleaning companies, they can focus 100% on graffiti removal as part of a niche or specialization strategy. Ideally, this should already be recognizable from the company name and an urgently recommended homepage. Painting companies could examine the extent to which they should include graffiti removal in the range of services as an additional element.

Competition and location analysis: take a close look!

So competition is not only represented by companies that have completely specialized in graffiti removal. Cleaning companies and painting companies must also appear on the analysis screen. A well-founded location and competition analysis must show how the demand is to be assessed and whether a differentiation strategy can be considered with the intended range of services. It has to be discussed whether the demand for graffiti removal at the location is resilient. Because there won't be a lively sprayer scene everywhere. It could be difficult in the country. One thing to keep in mind is that sprayers seek attention or a large audience with graffiti. Large cities are therefore an ideal business location for graffiti removal.

In the business plan, the scope of the business with all its resources (especially financial ones) must be very clear. The investments are kept within manageable limits. Because essentially a vehicle and work equipment are necessary for the start. Larger office space is not required, as customer advice can be given directly on site. Because of this initial situation, it is a business idea that can be considered without high sums of equity.

What legal form as an independent graffiti remover?

With the legal form, entrepreneurs set important questions concerning liability, corporate finance, and powers. Therefore, you should deal with various legal forms and their specific advantages before founding. Anyone who would like to try it as a lone wolf or self-employed person will usually operate as a sole proprietorship. If a larger cleaning company with several partners is to be founded, further partnerships or stock companies should be examined.

Graffiti Removal: How to Win Customers & Increase Sales?

Who are typical clients? In addition to private house and real estate owners, it is mainly companies who want to ensure an orderly appearance and do not tolerate graffiti in any form. In recent years, more and more public clients have been using the services of professional graffiti removers. These include schools, kindergartens, and public institutions (town halls, citizens' offices, museums, etc.). In marketing, independent graffiti removers can focus on a large target group or consciously position themselves for a very specific group. Anyone who positions themselves broadly in terms of performance and marketing will be able to ensure sustainable order acquisition. This is a very important aspect, especially in the financially critical start-up phase.

Use digital reach to increase awareness

In general, it is important to set up a professional graffiti remover with a long-range. A search engine optimized homepage is therefore essential to effectively automate the acquisition of orders in the start-up phase. The consideration of functional keywords must lead to customers searching via Google ending up on your website and ideally requesting an offer there.

High-reach or digital ways in customer acquisition

In the case of graffiti removal, interested customers can send in a picture of the unwanted graffiti to request a quote. Information on the size and the subsurface provide important information to be able to submit a sensibly calculated offer for customer acquisition.

Graffiti prophylaxis: Convincing added value in the range of services

What can you do preventively against graffiti or sprayers? The acquisition and, above all, the long-term loyalty of customers can be achieved through convincing added value in the service spectrum. In this sense, graffiti prophylaxis is a sensible offer. Professional graffiti removers can apply a special protective layer as a preventive measure. This can be temporary or permanent. If sprayers then try to perpetuate themselves, they will not be able to achieve the desired effects and removal will be a lot easier. In exposed locations, preventive measures can be a very convincing argument for customer acquisition. Service-oriented specialist advice on the best solution rounds off the holistic range of services from the customer's point of view. In the long run, such measures can take away sprayers' desire to perpetuate themselves. And if they take preventive measures, they must expect to be observed.

Requirements to become self-employed as a graffiti remover

Since this profession is not legally protected, no special qualifications are required. Without experience and knowledge of cleaning techniques and materials, business success will not be possible. After all, the work results are always immediately visible. And anyone who wants to use satisfied customers for advertising must be able to convince with professional quality at first glance.

Before self-employment, as a graffiti remover can be started, a business must be registered. In some federal states or cities, business registration is already possible online. Whether evidence has to be provided or authorization requirements have to be observed depends on the respective business operation and in particular on the specific range of services. The handling of special chemical cleaning agents undoubtedly requires a high level of expertise, which may need to be demonstrated with proof. Special knowledge will have to be proven if scaffolding has to be erected as part of the cleaning work on facades.

How much does a graffiti remover earn?

The business plan to be worked out must be able to answer this question realistically. Business start-ups have to show what income they can expect in the first few financial years and what costs will be offset against this.

In general, earnings as a graffiti remover largely depend on the following calculation variables: the size of the area to be processed, time factor, and use of materials and machines. When creating offers, start-ups should consider all these factors plus a profit margin. A high level of technical expertise is necessary for this to be able to correctly assess the time and effort required. Anyone who assumes 3 hours, but needs a whole working day, will have more than halved their earnings thanks to a fixed price for the customer. To earn a good income as a graffiti remover, the offer calculation must be very well thought out and profit-oriented from the start.

The other way round: Who pays for graffiti removal?

Unwanted graffiti: who pays the damage? After the initial anger is over, those affected are allowed to search for a professional service provider. This will initially pay the costs out of pocket. Based on Paragraph 823 of the Civil Code, those affected can sue the sprayer who caused the damage for damages. However, this option seldom works in practice, since most sprayers cannot be located. It should be checked in each case whether the building insurance will cover the costs. For most policies, this should not be the case. Corresponding options can certainly be provided in some high-performance tariffs. In any case, independent graffiti removers should also be able to give their customers professional advice on this issue to be able to convince them with a professional work ethic in every respect.

Practical tip: Check the special tax situation for commercial customers

A ruling by the Kassel regional court shows that the costs for graffiti removal can, under certain circumstances, be allocated to the operating cost category 'building cleaning'. According to the judgment, this option is only possible if these costs are incurred regularly.

Anyone self-employed as a graffiti remover should take out public liability insurance before starting a business. Even with the most careful way of working, objects can be damaged. To protect yourself from high claims for damages, there is no alternative to taking out public liability insurance from a financial point of view.

Summary & FAQ on the business idea 'become self-employed as a graffiti cleaner'

Why do you work as a graffiti cleaner?

Because it is an attractive target market because of sales volumes in the three-digit million range. Anyone who does not see graffiti from art will reflexively want to have it removed from the facade.

What are the advantages of this business idea or professional graffiti cleaning?

Without specialist knowledge, the necessary cleaning agents, and (high-pressure) devices, laypeople will quickly reach their limits or possibly visibly damage the surface. Against this background, professional graffiti removers must market their services with convincing added value.

How can customers be won over to graffiti cleaning?

With the highest possible digital reach, which must be ensured by a search engine optimized website. Traditional advertising materials such as flyers, radio advertising, newspaper advertisements, or vehicle advertising also continue to have a place in the marketing mix.

Which formal requirements do graffiti cleaners have to meet?

Anyone who becomes self-employed must register a business. With a view to the specific range of services, it must be checked whether evidence needs to be provided or whether a permit is required.

What can graffiti cleaners protect against business risks?

We urgently recommend that all business start-ups take out business liability insurance.

CONCLUSION

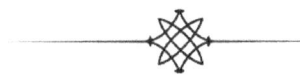

Anyone wanting to set up a cleaning company does not theoretically need any special training, but specific specialist knowledge, as well as commercial and business fundamentals, are essential to be successful in the long term. Also, you must be familiar with, among other things, health and safety at work and hazardous substances regulations. A coherent business concept and a viable business plan are the keys to ensuring that your cleaning company can defy the competition and operate profitably.

Therefore, analyze the market and your competitors and calculate your prices carefully. The financial plan helps you to keep track of your income and expenses and to convince financiers of the business concept of your cleaning company.

www.ingramcontent.com/pod-product-compliance
Lightning Source LLC
Chambersburg PA
CBHW020521111025
33889CB00011B/724